Ozark Country

Cajun Country
by Barry Jean Ancelet, Jay Edwards,
and Glen Pitre

Kentucky Bluegrass Country
by R. Gerald Alvey

Upper Cumberland Country
by William Lynwood Montell

South Florida Folklife
by Tina Bucuvalas, Peggy A. Bulger,
and Stetson Kennedy

Great Smoky Mountains
by Michael Ann Williams

William Lynwood Montell, General Editor

FOLKLIFE IN THE SOUTH SERIES

Ozark Country

W. K. McNeil

University Press of Mississippi Jackson

Manufactured in the United States of America

98 97 96 95   4 3 2 1

The paper in this book meets the guidelines for permanence
and durability of the Committee on Production Guidelines for
Book Longevity of the Council on Library Resources.

Library of Congress Cataloging-in-Publication Data

McNeil, W. K.
    Ozark country / W. K. McNeil
        p. cm.—(Folklife in the South series)
    Includes bibliographical references and index.
    ISBN 0-87805-728-5 (alk. paper).—ISBN 0-87805-729-3 (pbk.:
alk. paper)
        1. Ozark Mountains Region—Social life and customs. I. Title.
II. Series.
    F417.O9M36 1995
    976.7′1—dc20   95-14859
                                                   CIP

British Library Cataloging-in-Publication data available

To the Memory of Clay Anderson, 1931–1993

Contents

Folklife, a familiar concept in European scholarship for over a century, is the sum of a community's traditional forms of expression and behavior. It has claimed the attention of American folklorists since the 1950s. Each volume in the Folklife in the South Series focuses on the shared traditions that link people with their past and provide meaning and continuity for them in the present, and sets these traditions in the social contexts in which they flourish. Prepared by recognized scholars in various academic disciplines, these volumes are designed to be read separately. Each contains a vivid description of one region's traditional cultural element—ethnic and mainstream, rural and urban—that, in concert with those of other recognizable southern regions, lend a unique interpretation to the complex social structure of the South.

This comprehensive study of the Ozarks is the first such work since Vance Randolph's books in the early 1930s. Utilizing field research he and others have collected during the past two decades, W. K. McNeil goes beyond the survivalist approach of Randolph to show that Ozark folk culture is alive and well and constantly changing. He discusses historical folk culture and compares it to the current cultural traditions within this region, whose geographical boundaries include northern Arkansas, southern Missouri, and parts of Illinois, Kansas, and Oklahoma.

William Lynwood Montell
SERIES EDITOR

A c k n o w l e d g m e n t s

This survey of Ozark folk culture neither touches on every aspect of Ozark folklore nor covers any facet of the topic in great depth or detail. Instead, this brief examination is an attempt to show the breadth and diversity of Ozark folklore. Far from being a relatively simple, static phenomenon, Ozark folk culture, like that of any region, is complex and is constantly in a state of flux. In the sense of a uniform set of traditions followed by everyone in this mountain region, there is no such thing as Ozark folklore. Paradoxically, everyone in the Ozarks has folk traditions that are kept alive and transformed into newly evolving lore. Contrary to some popular stereotypes, it is not just the elderly who participate in these activities.

It is commonplace for folklore, Ozark or otherwise, to be accompanied by remarks about how the material has been collected from the last people who are keeping the traditions alive. My hope is that the following pages will show that such morbidity is unwarranted—that folklore is not only alive in the Ozarks but is flourishing there. It is true that some items pass out of existence, but others arise to take their place. For at least two hundred years the death of folklore has been predicted, but the subject refuses to die and seems unlikely to in the foreseeable future.

Ozark folklore provides solid evidence that, while the Ozarks has for much of its human history been geographically isolated, it has not been culturally isolated. Instead, like people everywhere, Ozarkers have been influenced by the culture of other areas, particularly by that of southern Appalachia. But traditions from elsewhere have not just been slavishly copied; they have been translated into similar, yet new, forms. That is why, culturally speaking, the Ozarks is not Appalachia West or, for that matter, a carbon copy of any other region.

It would be desirable but impossible to list every person who has influenced my thinking on Ozark culture. I will mention here only those who specifically contributed to the present book. These include Desmond Walls Allen, Sarah Brown, James Denny, Gerald Dupy, Robert K. Gilmore, Bob Hammack, James Johnston, Gordon McCann, William McCarthy, Lynn Morrow, Phyllis Rossiter, Barbara Wehrman, and George West. They are, of course, in no way to be held responsible for interpretations.

Authors of books such as this survey of Ozark folklore are, in a sense, perpetuating a fiction, but that is necessary if there is to be a cohesive manuscript. Namely, such books present a picture of a nonexistent unity throughout the region under discussion. Certainly, at no particular time did every single Ozark resident from one end of the region to the other engage in all the activities discussed herein. Even all those involved in the same skill or craft didn't necessarily go about it in exactly the same way but in most cases added their own innovative touches to whatever they did. But any folklorist or historian must impose some notion of unity in order to have a book that does not seem to be made up of disparate parts. Thus, with *Ozark Country*, such an illusion is conferred, even though in reality things were never so uniform.

In an attempt to make the book both interesting and informative to nonspecialist audiences, the volume is broken down in three segments: home, work, and leisure. Chapter 2, "Family Ties," discusses traditional arts and crafts that in the early years of Ozark history were made in or at one's homeplace. This is not to suggest that these skills have invariably been practiced only at home; in fact, today such crafts are as likely to be demonstrated at county fairs, museums, arts and crafts shows, and similar venues as in the home. Nevertheless, the primary forum for soapmaking, clothing, foodways, and even furniture making originally was the home and, in most cases, it still is.

Chapter 3, "At Work," examines such skills as blacksmithing, pottery making, and gun making that have traditionally been practiced away from home in some kind of work place. The production of these items served primarily to provide a living for their practitioners, although there were some, known in the Ozarks as "jacklegs," who knew a little bit about these crafts and occasionally made or fixed certain products, although never for monetary gain. Some other skills, such as pearling, were mostly regarded as a means of providing supplemental income rather than being a family's sole source of funds. A few craft items, such as the Ozark john-boat, were unique to the region, but most Ozark craftsmen produced items known elsewhere, although these frequently incorporated subtle touches that can accurately be considered indigenous to the Ozarks.

Chapter 4 deals with various types of folk customs that have been or are now observed in the Ozarks. The majority of these are either concerned with rites of passage or are calendar customs. Some, such as the dumb supper, probably seem exotic to modern readers, while infares, which linger on as part of shivarees, may not seem unusual even though they are extinct, since they are strongly reminiscent of current practices. The practice of observing calendar customs provides a useful argument to those who regard Ozark folk culture as duplicating what is found in Appalachia, because, except in minor details, the traditions in the two regions do not vary appreciably. The chapter includes a discussion of folk medicine, an important but relatively little-considered aspect of Ozark folk tradition. While not part of folk custom but of belief, these practices are a closely related although distinctly different part of folklore.

The last three chapters of *Ozark Country* have to do with leisure time traditions. For many people, folk music, ballads and folksongs are the most important component of folklore, a bias that has arisen largely because these subjects have occupied the attention of many folklorists in the past. My aim in the present work is to illustrate that there are many aspects of leisure time folk traditions found in the Ozarks, including various kinds of games and entertainments and the use of folk narratives.

CHAPTER 1

Historical Overview

The Ozarks are perhaps unique among major mountain regions in that many of the important questions about this formation cannot be answered precisely, or, in some cases, at all. For example, it would seem easy enough to define the specific area covered by the mountains, but instead the extent of the range changes according to who is doing the describing. Ask any two experts to tell you where the geographical boundaries of the Ozarks are, and you are likely to receive two different answers. In the most liberal definition, the Ozarks include most of northern Arkansas, southern Missouri, eastern Oklahoma, a small section of eastern Kansas, and a small portion of southern Illinois; the most exclusive definition allows only most of northern Arkansas and southern Missouri. If the most inclusive drawing of lines is chosen, then it can be said that the Ozarks are bounded in a rough way by major rivers: the Missouri on the north, the Mississippi on the east, the Arkansas on the south, and the Neosho on the west. By any measure the region is a vast one, consisting of more than sixty thousand square miles.

There is also disagreement about the name "Ozark," which first appeared in English in reference to the mountain range. According to most explanations, it is an Anglicization of a French phrase, but there is disagreement about which one. According to one hypothesis, the term is derived from the French phrase *bois aux arcs*, which refers to a wood used for bows. When the first Europeans—Frenchmen—came into the Ozarks, they noted that the Indians used bows and arrows that were unusually strong. These were made from the wood of the bois d'arc tree (also known as the Osage orange or the hedge apple); upon learning this fact, the French trappers called the entire region "Bois aux Arcs." After some time the term was shortened to "Aux Arcs" and eventually Anglicized to the present "Ozarks."

A second theory connects the name to a geological thesis popular around the time of the American Revolution. Abraham Gottlob Werner, a German scientist, suggested that there were two kinds of rock formations found in the earth: aqueous rock formed by the action of water and containing fossils, and azoic rock formed by fire that contained no living organisms. Several of the Europeans who first came into the region were

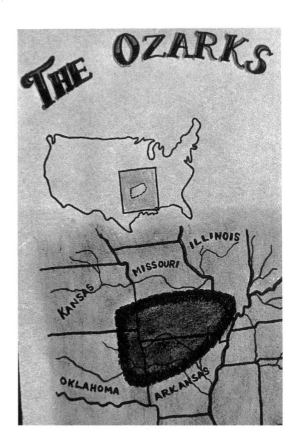

Map of Ozarks (Photo
from author's collection)

aware of Werner's ideas and called the granite rocks found throughout the
area "azoic." On a map this territory roughly resembles an arc, especially
according to the more inclusive set of geographical boundaries, and so
this became the "Azoic Arc," a name that ultimately evolved into the
present "Ozark."

The third theory, and the one that most people accept, holds that the
name is derived from the tendency of early French settlers to abbreviate
long Indian tribal names by using only the first syllables. For example,
documents might refer to a hunting expedition of fur traders as "aux
Kans," meaning into the territory of the Kansas Tribe. Thus the French
would have used the terms "aux Os" and "aux Arks" to refer to excursions
into the territory of the Osage and Arkansas Indians, and the two terms
were eventually Anglicized to become "Ozarks."

While there is dispute about the origins of the name, there is no argument about its first gaining widespread acceptance in the early nineteenth
century. In 1809 John Bradbury, an English traveler, became the first
person to use the word "Ozark" in print. Six years later, in 1815, government explorer Stephen H. Long used the name "Ozark Mountains" on a

map, and he is generally credited with making the name official. In 1821 Henry Rowe Schoolcraft, who was a famous explorer and writer as well as the "father of American folklore scholarship," published a book in which he referred to the region as the Ozarks. This volume, *Journal of a Tour into the Interior of Missouri and Arkansas in 1818 and 1819*, recounted a journey undertaken in search of lead mines and also included a few examples of Ozark folklore. Over three decades later, in 1853, Schoolcraft produced *Scenes and Adventures in the Semi-Alpine Regions of the Ozark Mountains of Missouri and Arkansas*, which gave further details about his explorations in 1818 and 1819. By this time "Ozark" was in common usage, with Schoolcraft deserving some of the credit for popularizing the name outside the region.

What are the cultural traits that distinguish the Ozarks? The major one is that the region is rural. In *The Ozarks: Land and Life* (p. 4), Milton Rafferty suggests that this "is the least argumentative and perhaps the most important cultural fact relating to the Ozarks." There are, of course, some urban sections—for example, Springfield and Joplin in Missouri and the Fayetteville-Springdale-Rogers area in Arkansas—but the general nature of daily life in the Ozarks is rural. Even most of the tourist-oriented communities, such as Eureka Springs, Arkansas, and Branson, Missouri, are small towns, most having populations of well under ten thousand.

A second distinctive feature is the Ozarker's sense of place. While experts may not agree on exactly where the geographical boundaries of the Ozarks are, the people who live in the region do not hesitate to identify themselves as Ozarkers and recent arrivals as outsiders. In many communities, natives consider those not born in the Ozarks to be outsiders even though they may have spent all but a few years of their lives in the region. Frequently, outsiders are referred to as persons "from off."

Another cultural trait characteristic of the Ozarks is a relatively stable social system, especially compared to those found in most other parts of the United States. There are strong, secure kinship relations extending back for generations, and social activities are centered around schools and churches, institutions that are dependable and predictable. Friends and enemies are clearly defined, and Ozarkers know what to do about both groups.

A final aspect of Ozark culture that deserves mention is the role that Upland South immigrants and their descendants have played in shaping the traditional heritage of the Ozarks. Migrants from eastern Tennessee, southeastern Kentucky, southwestern Virginia, and other parts of southern Appalachia were not the earliest settlers in the Ozarks, but they have been the largest and most influential group. It is because of this influx from the mountains to the east and the prominent role played in Ozark culture by these settlers that the region is often viewed as being little more than Appalachia West.

The Ozarks and the southern Appalachian Mountains are often linked in both popular and scholarly thought, frequently being viewed in stereotypical ways by those who should know better. Historian Arnold Toynbee (*A Study of History*, I, p. 149) gives this assessment of Appalachia:

If we compare the Ulsterman and the Appalachian of to-day, two centuries after they parted company, we shall find that . . . the modern Appalachian has not only not improved on the Ulsterman; he has failed to hold his ground and has gone downhill in a most disconcerting fashion. In fact, the Appalachian 'mountain people' to-day are no better than barbarians. They have relapsed into illiteracy and witchcraft. They suffer from poverty, squalor and ill-health. They are the American counterparts of the latter-day White barbarians of the Old World— Rifis, Albanians, Kurds, Pathans and Hairy Ainus; but, whereas these latter are belated survivals of an ancient barbarism, the Appalachians present the melancholy spectacle of a people who have acquired civilization and then lost it.

Toynbee was silent on inhabitants of the Ozark mountains but it is unlikely that he held them in higher esteem than he did Appalachian mountaineers; certainly, some others didn't. John Gunther, in *Inside U. S. A.* (1947)—a book praised by Arthur M. Schlesinger, Jr., and Henry Steele Commager, among others, as intelligent, perceptive, and objective reporting—has this to say about the Ozarks: "The Ozarks are a world in themselves. Perhaps, oddly, there is little mineral wealth in the Ozarks except zinc and lead; the oil, I heard it put, 'drained out to Kansas a couple of million years ago.' There is not so much human wealth either. The Ozarks are the Poor White Trash citadel of America. The people are undeveloped, suspicious, and inert. There are children aged fifteen who have never seen a toothbrush" (p. 342).

Some other writers who are more moderate in their comments also think of the two mountain regions as essentially the same. Richard M. Dorson, in a chapter on Appalachian mountaineers in his book *Buying the Wind* (a collection of traditional lore from seven distinctive American folk regions), says, "The Ozark hillman closely resembles the southern mountaineer [i.e., the southern Appalachian mountaineer], and in fact the Arkansas uplands were largely settled in the early decades of the nineteenth century by migrant Appalachian folk" (p. 166). Dorson, of course, is correct in his statement that a substantial portion of early Ozark settlement was carried out by people from Appalachia. He is also undoubtedly correct in his assumption that much Ozark folklore is basically the same as that found in southern Appalachia. But, as this book will show, it is inaccurate to claim that the Ozarks are merely Appalachia West. Those who do so make the erroneous assumption that no other cultural groups had any significant impact on the region. In fact, three major groups had periods of cultural dominance in the Ozarks before the major wave of migrants from southern Appalachia in the mid-nineteenth century. Of these the earliest were American Indians.

AMERICAN INDIANS

Exactly when tribal groups first entered the region now called the Ozarks is unknown, but they were definitely there by 12,000 B.C. Relatively little is known about the earliest hunting groups, but the distribution of various archaeological sites suggests that they were exploiting natural resources found in the Missouri and Mississippi river valleys. Although they were primarily hunters, their food supply also included seeds, roots, and fruits. The bow and arrow were apparently unknown, and weapons were made from native chert. Open-air villages and campsites were located on hilltops or high terraces near a permanent water supply. The people lived in caves and natural rock shelters, but whether or not they built houses is unknown.

About 1,000 B.C. tribal groups living in the Ozarks developed a type of crude but functional pottery. This pottery was made from clay, sand, crushed bone, or crushed limestone. About the same time the practice of building low mounds for burial of the dead was initiated, and ceremonial smoking with pipes became commonplace. During this era the bow and arrow first became generally used in hunting, and tribal groups began to cultivate small gardens. Whereas the earlier tribal groups in the Ozarks were nomadic, after about 1,000 B.C. they became more sedentary and more inclined to farm, although hunting still played a major role in procuring food.

A new period of Indian life in the Ozarks developed about A.D. 900, although it did not exhibit the marked changes found in other areas. For example, in the southeastern United States and Mississippi Valley, people

Indian Settlement of the Ozarks

PERIOD	DURATION	CHARACTERISTICS
Paleo-Indian Period	12,000 B.C.—8,000 B.C.	Early hunter
Dalton Period	8,000 B.C.—7,000 B.C.	Hunter-forager
Archaic Period	7,000 B.C.—1,000 B.C.	Forager
Woodland Period	1,000 B.C.—A.D. 900	Prairie-forest potter
Mississippian Period	A.D. 900—A.D. 1700	Village farmer
Historic Period	A.D. 1700—A.D. 1835	European contact

lived in fortified villages consisting of permanent thatched-roof houses, square or rectangular in shape, and having wattle-and-daub walls. Moreover, the southeastern and Mississippi Valley Indians were primarily agriculturalists who lived in permanent villages. Large ceremonial mounds were commonplace, pottery making became more fully developed, and extensive trade was conducted with tribes living along the Gulf Coast. Except for those people living at the edge of the mountain range, these developments were basically unknown by most tribes in the Ozarks. There are many possible explanations as to why the changes wrought during this era made little impression on Ozark Indians, including a paucity of people and resources, difficulty of travel in the region, and a tenacious resistance to change on the part of these Indians. Interestingly, these interpretations are still offered to this day by many seeking to explain the special nature of the Ozarks.

The years from 1700 to 1835, the era of European contact, marked the end of Indian occupation of the Ozarks. This does not mean that no Indians lived in the region after that, but that they ceased to represent a dominant culture. This period was marked by permanent villages, well-crafted and decorated pots, extensive trade with the French, greater use of the horse, and more rapid change in Indian culture. When Indians found that some of the European goods were superior to their own, many of their traditional arts and crafts fell into disuse. Also during this period the United States government attempted to dispossess the Indians and remove them to increasingly smaller land reserves farther west. The Trail of Tears is the most famous result of these efforts.

There were numerous tribal groups in the Ozarks. Most of the Indians that moved from the East to west of the Mississippi River spent some time in these mountains, but in the years from 1700 to 1835 the four major tribes in the region were the Osage, Illinois, Caddos, and Quapaws. The most important of these were the Osage, who, by 1800, had laid claim to the major portion of the Ozark Plateau, with their territory extending from the Missouri River on the north to the Arkansas River on the south and from the Mississippi River on the east to the western prairies. In 1805 one traveler estimated that they had the ability to raise a thousand warriors. (*Indians of the Ozark Plateau*, p. 59).

In 1808 the Osage ceded their claims to a major portion of the Ozarks in their first treaty with the United States government. In a document signed at Fort Osage, about twenty miles east of present-day Kansas City, the Osage relinquished their land between the Missouri and Arkansas rivers east of a line running due south from Fort Osage to the Arkansas River. Contending that they had given up the land but not their right to hunt there, they continued to do so long afterward. Although generally peaceful, the Osage occasionally raided white settlements, taking scalps and slaves not only from those inhabitants but from various other Indian tribes living in the Ozarks.

The Illinois Indians lived along the Mississippi River at the edge of the Ozarks, the Quapaws occupied a small part of the southeastern Ozarks, and the Caddos hunted throughout the Arkansas and southwest Missouri Ozarks. After the Louisiana Purchase in 1803, a number of eastern Indians moved into the region, and even before that several tribes, including the Kickapoos, Shawnees, Delawares, and Cherokees had migrated into the Ozarks. The Spanish, who had owned the region for several years before 1803, thought that a friendly Indian population would help them retain possession of their lands west of the Mississippi River; thus, they facilitated the migration of various tribes into the territory. The most important of these immigrant tribes in the eighteenth and nineteenth centuries was the Cherokees.

The first Cherokees to settle west of the Mississippi moved as a result of the Treaty of Hopewell in 1785. Unhappy with the treaty's terms, a few Cherokees traveled on the Tennessee, Ohio, and Mississippi rivers to establish settlements near the St. Francis and White rivers in northeastern Arkansas. Approximately two decades later, Thomas Jefferson encouraged a group of Cherokees to send a delegation to inspect lands in the Arkansas Territory with the intention of exchanging part of this region for their home area east of the Mississippi. After a favorable report on the new territory, over two thousand Cherokees, seeking to exchange their agricultural economy for one based on hunting, moved into the Arkansas Ozarks. By 1819 there were over thirty-five hundred Cherokees living in the region. Two years earlier, in 1817, the Cherokees had signed a treaty with the United States that gave them a large tract of land that included the Boston Mountains. The eastern boundary extended northeastward from a point near the present city of Morrilton to the White River near Batesville, while the western boundary, undecided until 1825, began ten miles north of Fort Smith and ran northeastward paralleling the eastern boundary to the White River. The southern and northern boundaries were, respectively, the Arkansas and White rivers.

While the Cherokees were pleased with the terms of this treaty, the white settlers living in the region were not. In his 1818 journey down the White River, Henry Rowe Schoolcraft encountered evidence of local discontent directed toward the Cherokees in the person of a Mrs. John Lafferty. The widow of one of the first white settlers above Batesville, she told Schoolcraft that she and her immediate neighbors were very upset with the treaty. They specifically objected to being forced to give up farms that they had improved and where they had lived for several years. At the time she met Schoolcraft, Mrs. Lafferty was making plans to move across the river to a farm in what is now Izard County. Fourteen years later, in 1832, she died on that farm.

On May 6, 1828, the Cherokees exchanged their land in the Arkansas Ozarks for seven million choice acres north of the Arkansas River in Indian Territory. Within a year most of the Cherokees living in Arkansas moved to this new home area to escape harassment by white settlers. Those members of the tribe living along the White River were more reluctant to move, and several years later, in the mid-1830s, many of these Cherokees remained on their unimproved claims. Most of these Indians moved to the western Ozarks in the late 1830s at the time of the Trail of Tears, being joined by a large body of Eastern Cherokees. Several of the Cherokees on the Upper White River remained behind because they had intermarried with the early white settlers. Descendants of those marriages still live in the region; many current residents of the White River country proudly trace their families back to a Cherokee ancestor.

Although the period of Indian dominance in the Ozarks was over by 1840, the tribes left a legacy that is reflected in various ways in contemporary Ozark culture. Frequently, Indians serve a symbolic function, as in the numerous pseudo-Indian place names and place name legends. Some, such as Wasola in Ozark County, Missouri, are merely white attempts to create an Indian-sounding name. In a book by Ernie Deane, the following account is given of how Spadra, in Johnson County, Arkansas, got its name: "One Pedro supposedly made his way west of the Mississippi ahead of Hernando de Soto, and to the Quapaw Indians where he and the chief's daughter, Coree, fell in love. Unable to marry, because of the father's objections, the couple tried to run away, but were overtaken. Coree was killed by a spear in protecting her lover. He, in turn, broke his sword in the fight and was killed. In later years, the legend holds, DeSoto [*sic*] found the sword, cried 'spadra,' supposedly meaning 'broken sword,' and thus the name of the place and the creek was established" (*Arkansas Place Names*, p. 124).

The Indian as a symbolic figure is seen in many other aspects of Ozark culture, such as the once-popular children's game of Indians and Pioneers. Another example involves numerous narratives that were once common in the Ozarks about a mysterious, generic figure named Indian Joe. According to these legends, Indian Joe and his squaw stayed behind when other Indians moved farther west. They lived variously at an isolated cabin site, a spring, or a cave, and after their deaths these places were haunted by Indian spirits capable of scalping or committing other violent deeds. Symbolic Indians also appear in such "Indian" songs as "Red Wing," the melody of which is derived from a classical tune, and in a square dance called "Indian Style." This folk dance, an attempt to imitate Indian dancing—or what is believed to be Indian-style dancing—also includes loud war whoops at periodic intervals.

The Indian cultural legacy is not entirely symbolic; some place names are derived from actual Indian names, such as the Kickapoo Prairie, where Springfield, Missouri, is located. Taum Sauk, the highest mountain in Missouri, is named for the Sauks, one of the numerous tribes that spent some time in the Ozarks. Neosho, the name of a river and of a Missouri town, is a Siouan term meaning "main river." Hi Wassie, a name given to communities in Missouri and Arkansas, is the Cherokee word for "meadow."

FRENCH

The period of white contact with Indians in the Ozarks began in about 1700, when the French moved into the region. Although their earliest forays into the area were farther south, their first settlements were in the northeastern section of the Ozarks near St. Louis. In 1673 the French explorers Jacques Marquette and Louis Joliet reached the mouth of the Arkansas River at the southern boundary of the Ozarks. Nine years later, in 1682, Sieur de La Salle visited the village of the Quapaws in present-day Arkansas, and in 1686 La Salle's lieutenant, Henri de Tonty, leading an expedition in quest of his missing leader, established Arkansas Post near the site where the Arkansas and White rivers merge. It was, however, the desire for furs and minerals that was of primary importance in the French occupation of the Ozarks. Missionaries, the earliest French settlers, were soon joined by fur traders, soldiers, and farmers. Their travel was primarily by way of the Mississippi River, which was the main link between the major French settlements on the Great Lakes and in Louisiana. The eastern Ozarks was almost in the middle of the vast French domain, and, in the five decades following the Marquette and Joliet expedition, several permanent French settlements were established in this area, which was made attractive by fertile soil, favorable growing conditions, and a sufficient supply of fur-bearing animals. Equally important was the discovery of lead deposits in the Ozarks, which had occurred by 1700. Two years into the century, patents to work the mines were sought. In 1704, Sieur de Bienville, French governor of Louisiana, reported that the French had settled west of the Mississippi in the Ozarks.

During the first three decades of the eighteenth century, a number of French communities were established in the Ozarks. In 1714 Antoine de la Mothe Cadillac, founder of Detroit and then governor general of Louisiana, discovered mines one hundred miles south of St. Louis, and, in 1723, Mine La Motte was named for him. The following year Bonne

Terre was established a few miles away; the name, a French phrase meaning "good land," was descriptive of the area in general. In subsequent years Old Mines and many other French mining communities were founded. These villages prospered and grew slowly but steadily over the next several decades.

While the French had considerably more in the way of material goods than most of the Indians who preceded them in the Ozarks, they still did not have a privileged life. Most of the people were illiterate; there were few luxuries, and even such seemingly essential items as spinning wheels were rare. However, the French population was generally prosperous, if not wealthy, and enjoyed a peaceful life-style. This group represented the dominant cultural force in the region for well over a century, although, except for place names and a few architectural sites, little French imprint is evident in the present-day Ozarks. A few French customs, such as the New Year's Eve practice of *La Guignolee*, are currently practiced, but in almost every instance they are recent revivals of long-dormant activities.

GERMANS

Unlike the French, the Germans who migrated into the Ozarks were greatly concerned with preserving their Old World culture. In fact, the Hermann Colony, the largest single German colony in Missouri and the Ozarks, was originally intended to be the nucleus of a German state. The plan died when it was not approved by either the state of Missouri or the United States government. However, the Germans continued to make a special effort to preserve their native language and many of their institutions. This could best be accomplished when the population was homogeneous; thus, they tended to move into areas that were already settled by Germans or that were unsettled, where compact, well-organized communities could be established. Their migration tendencies meant that they were often situated on land of relatively low quality, but because they were willing to accept such acreage, they were able to purchase large adjoining blocks of land. Control of land remains an important consideration in most German communities in the Ozarks even today. Land changes hands very slowly, and when it does it usually goes from one German to another. This situation contrasts with the norm elsewhere in the Ozarks. Such cohesiveness enabled Germans to preserve their native language and institutions to a greater extent than is the case with most ethnic groups in the Ozarks.

Until the time of World War Two, the German language was commonly spoken in Ozark German communities. Although at that time it became politically unwise to promote the language, it never completely died out. For several years private schools were the primary means of teaching German. (In some communities most of the children attended parochial schools, making those more important and influential than the public schools.) That older residents never gave up their native language is recognized by some churches; many rural Lutheran churches, for example, offer services in German on an irregular basis.

The major wave of German immigration in the Ozarks occurred from 1830 to 1850, with settlements being established primarily in the northern and eastern portions of the mountains. These migrants were of four major types: romanticists, religious separatists, members of the *Jungdeutschland* movement, and people seeking to better their economic situation. Some were hoping to escape government or religious oppression, while others were merely looking for a society more interesting and exotic than the one they had left behind. A book written by Gottfried Duden in 1829, *Berich über eine Reise nach den westlichen Staaten Nordamerikas (Report on a Journey to the Western States of North America)* bore considerable responsibility for bringing Germans to the Ozarks. Indeed, Marcus Lee Hansen has called this book the "most important piece of literature in the history of German emigration" (*The Atlantic Migration 1607–1860*, p. 149). Duden's account of the northern Ozarks was often Edenic, but his advice was not totally unrealistic. For example, he noted that "emigration of individuals without leadership and medical protection is to be considered a great risk" (Duden, 1980, p. 246). In most respects, though, he painted a glowing picture of the Ozarks as a place having many of the virtues of Germany without the liabilities.

Besides the language and numerous place names in the northern and eastern Ozarks, other evidence of German influence is found in several festivals and celebrations. The best-known example is the Maifest held annually in Hermann, Missouri, where German music, dancing, and food constitute a blend of traditional and popular culture. The town's ambiance is important, too, as the German-style architecture has a decidedly Old World feel. In her recent guidebook, Phyllis Rossiter proclaims that Hermann remains "more like nineteenth-century Germany than Germany itself. A visit to Hermann today affords the traveler a glimpse . . . of the Europe of nearly two centuries ago" (*A Living History of the Ozarks*, p. 25).

While there has been more assimilation in the past thirty years than in the previous century, Germans still have been more successful at maintaining their traditions than most other ethnic groups in the Ozarks. Ironically, this success has meant that German influence on Ozark culture in general has been relatively minor. Their settlement patterns, agriculture, and religion represent the major contributions. Relatively little from their oral traditions has come into common usage throughout the region.

AFRICAN-AMERICANS

Black Americans of African ancestry constitute one of the smaller migrant groups in the Ozarks and the one least often associated with the region in popular thought. Their numbers have never been large, but they were among the earliest non-Indian people in the area, although, of course, they did not come of their own volition. In 1719 Phillippe Renault brought five hundred slaves to labor in his mines in the eastern Ozarks. While in subsequent years a few other slaveholders found their way into the mountains, at no time were there huge numbers of slaves, and most slaveholders had only a single slave. Before the Civil War most of the black population of the Ozarks was concentrated along the major rivers and in the mining districts.

Primarily for economic and social reasons, the black population of the Ozarks declined sharply after the Civil War. Because they owned no land and there were few opportunities for employment, and because of white hostility, many young blacks left the region. This population declined steadily until 1930, by which time six Ozark counties had no blacks and many others had fewer than a dozen. At the present time blacks constitute less than 2 percent of the Ozark population, with most living in the region's urban areas or border counties.

OTHER EUROPEAN ETHNIC AND CULTURAL GROUPS

Just about every cultural and ethnic group that found its way to other parts of the United States is represented to some extent in the Ozarks. In some cases such as Poles, Swiss, Swedes, Italians, and several others, the representation is very small, consisting usually of a few sparsely populated communities. Many of these ethnic groups came to the region as a result of colonization programs carried out by railroad companies in the immediate post–Civil War years. Sometimes the railroad companies sent agents or advertisements to Europe to solicit immigrants. The experience of the Waldensians was typical. They were a Christian sect who had long suffered religious persecution in their native home in the Cottian Alps on the French-Italian border. Many Waldensians who sought asylum immigrated to Switzerland and Germany. One group went to Uruguay in the 1850s. Concerned with violence and repeated revolutions there, the colony was enticed to relocate in Missouri by the advertisements of the Atlantic and Pacific Railroad, the parent company of the St. Louis-San Francisco Railroad Company. They selected a forested location near Monett instead of on the fertile prairie (later known as the Freistatt Prairie), because having lived in Uruguay where wood was scarce, they felt an abundance of wood was a great advantage to settlement. Originally, nine families from Uruguay established the colony in 1875; later, more than twenty families emigrated from Europe to the Monett settlement.

Most of the small European ethnic groups that migrated to the Ozarks were united as much by religion as ethnicity. This is particularly true in the case of the Amish and Mennonites, who trace their origins back to sixteenth-century Europe in the era following the Protestant Reformation. Both groups were Anabaptists, which meant that they denied the validity of infant baptism and emphasized adult baptism. They also believed in the separation of church and state and wanted absolute freedom in religious affairs. They were opposed to bearing arms, swearing, or any other activities that they felt departed from the peaceful example of Christ. For such beliefs they were persecuted and tortured, eventually fleeing to North America. Initially they moved to or near Philadelphia, but over the course of many decades a large number migrated to the Corn Belt and the Great Plains.

Although there were Mennonites in the Ozarks as early as 1850 and the Amish were there by 1890, most of their settlements in the region date from the 1960s. Several factors led to this recent migration, of which two are paramount. One was that the older areas of Amish-Mennonite settlement were becoming so crowded that it was impossible for everyone to be engaged in farming. The second was that land in those older areas of settlement was becoming prohibitively expensive, making outmigration a desirable alternative. The Ozarks was appealing because land was relatively inexpensive, and the potential for future expansion of land holdings was good. Related considerations were that laws regarding education and public schools were more in line with the needs of the Amish and Mennonites, and the idea of the area's isolation, even though inaccurate, was appealing.

While both groups adhere to old ways, it is the Amish who do so most closely. Their style of dress, their rejection of the automobile and other modern conveniences, and even their manner of worship suggest a past age. Being so concerned with isolating themselves from other groups and their ways has meant that both the Amish and Mennonites have influenced the traditions of those outside their own communities relatively little. For exactly opposite reasons the same conclusion can be made about most of the other small European ethnic groups in the Ozarks. Instead of isolating themselves from their neighbors, the Swiss, Poles, and Swedes frequently intermarried with outsiders, thereby weakening the ethnic ties. Within a relatively short time, pronounced cultural characteristics associated with these groups disappeared. Today, remaining place names such as Altus, Arkansas, and Swedeborg, Missouri, represent their main contribution to Ozark culture.

SOUTHERN APPALACHIAN MIGRANTS

By far the most influential group of immigrants in the Ozarks came from the Upland South, primarily from east Tennessee, eastern Kentucky, southwestern Virginia, and western North Carolina. Most of these people are called Scotch-Irish, a label that is misleading. It is based on the un-proven assumption that a distinct ethnic group that remained racially pure for many generations settled the southern Appalachians and later moved into the Ozarks. This theory has been based on such questionable approaches as the study of surnames in southern Appalachia, a suspect undertaking because the names of many people were changed over the years. It can be assumed that these inhabitants came from the British Isles, since English was the main language spoken, but at this time it is probably impossible to prove definitively that they were descendants of people from Scotland and northern Ireland. In any case, they had blended in so well with other Americans that any specific ethnic makeup was for-gotten, or at least not particularly important to them.

However, there is no doubt that migrants from the Upland South started moving into the Ozarks in the nineteenth century. Actually, these people had stayed in southern Appalachia a short time, as the first perma-nent non-Indian settlements there dated only from the 1750s. There are many possible explanations of their move to the Ozarks. The early nine-teenth century was a time when many Americans were moving westward. In 1790 five percent of America's people lived west of the Appalachians; sixty years later, in 1850, nearly half the population resided west of that mountain range. Although migrants from the Upland South had ventured into the Ozarks earlier, their movement intensified during the two dec-ades immediately preceding the Civil War. It is a truism that when leav-ing a region many people tend to move to a place comparable to the one they left. The Ozarks was the first place nineteenth-century Appalachian mountaineers found that looked like what had been home, so they de-cided to stay. Of course, not all Appalachian migrants remained in the Ozarks. For many it was just a temporary stop, and eventually they con-tinued their movement to the central Texas hills, the northern Rockies, or the Cascades of Oregon and Washington.

A compelling reason for the migration from Appalachia to the Ozarks was the availability of land. In Appalachia many people, including Daniel Boone (who spent his last years in Missouri), were unable to secure land titles, so for them the Ozarks with its available land was a desirable place to settle. A further motivation was that land bounties were available to veterans of the Revolutionary War and War of 1812 and their descendants. The Upland South migrants first settled in the larger, more accessible valleys and then in smaller, more isolated areas. After passage of a graduation act in the 1850s, many people from Appalachia moved into the more remote sections of the Ozarks. This act provided for the lowering of prices on land that was not selling until it eventually did.

It is also undoubtedly true that some people moved from southern Appalachia into the Ozarks for reasons similar to the one that motivated a schoolteacher profiled by early Ozark collector of folklore and oral history Silas C. Turnbo and included in the collection edited by Desmond Walls Allen:

In the winter of 1860–1861, a man who called himself William Sears taught school in a small log house that stood on the bank of a hollow just on the east side of Shoal Creek in Keesee Township, Marion County, Arkansas. . . . It turned out that the teacher's name was not Sears, but William Evens was his proper name, and he formerly lived in the state of Tennessee, that he killed a man there and fled to White River and changed his name to Sears. Sears had a little boy named Edward who went to school with his father on Shoal Creek. Reports had it that, when Sears shot the man in Tennessee, the man had first tried to shoot Sears through a window and he snatched up his child Edward who was an infant then and placed him in the window and held him there and the man did not shoot. This gave Sears time to jerk his pistol from his belt and prepare it for shooting, and he shot and killed the man (in *Turnbo's Tales of the Ozarks: Biographical Stories*, p. 14).

Such stories are familiar in most frontier areas and do not apply to a major portion of the region's early population.

Certainly many Appalachian migrants moved into the Ozarks to join other members of their families. This was, in effect, a chain migration in which the first family members to arrive sent word to relatives, who then came. The moving of large extended families into the same sections of the Ozarks over several decades was not uncommon. Regardless of the reasons for their move, migrants from the Upland South exercised a cultural influence in their new home region far greater than that of any other ethnic or cultural group. For that reason it is primarily their folk traditions and culture that are examined in the following pages.

CHAPTER 2

Family Ties

Ozark life-styles may be generally classified as traditional or nontraditional, with the former obviously being of primary concern here. Families and family life are very important to most traditional Ozarkers, and knowing family genealogy is considered important. People take great pride in their family trees, although it is usually not possible to go back farther than four generations. Even today, young and old alike frequently identify themselves by mentioning their parents' names. Cultural geographer Milton D. Rafferty, of Southwest Missouri State University in Springfield, once received firsthand evidence of this pride in family history: "I recall stopping at a house to inquire about directions to a place and, after a while, the conversation somehow was sidetracked into family history. A son, fortyish, recently returned from fifteen years of military service, gave a recitation on the family tree, including several divorces, stepchildren, half-brothers and sisters, cousins, nephews, and nieces while his mother looked on, nodding her head in approving fashion" (in *The Ozarks: Land and Life*, p. 240).

This interest in family extends to the entire community, with people often being identified through their relatives, particularly when those relatives might be better established locally. Unlike the stereotype of the noncommunicative, isolationist Ozarker, the hillfolk are interested in and knowledgeable about their neighbors. Silas Turnbo had little difficulty collecting numerous detailed narratives such as the following:

I am a son of Ambrose Yancy and Sidney (Jones) Stone and was born in Maries County, Missouri, April 23, 1842. The locality where my parents lived when I was born was on Little Tavern Creek which flows into Big Tavern. The last named stream goes into the Gasconade River. . . . Bobby Rowden built the first mill in our neighborhood which was built on Rowden's Creek. This stream took its name from the Rowden family and runs into Little Tavern Creek. The mill was a small affair and ground corn only. I remember all these people and the mill when I was near six years of age. One of my father's brothers, Rig (Gilmore) Stone and his wife, Aunt Celia, also lived in our neighborhood.

John Stone was my grandfather. He was born in Wales in 1755, and soon after he was grown, he came to the United States and finally shifted to Missouri where he died in Maries County in 1851, at the age of 96 years. He was buried in a

Vance Randolph, premier folklorist of the Ozarks (Photo courtesy Ozark Folk Center)

graveyard on Big Maries Creek. . . . Colonel Johnson, who bore that title when I could first remember him, was from Virginia. Tom Kinzie built the first mill on a small creek that empties into the Gasconade River. The mill was operated by a spring that formed the creek. The mill stood one-half mile from the river and the spring run out of the ground in the hollow a short distance above the mill. There were also David Hoops and Miskel Johnson. The last named served in the Confederate Army as an officer.

The first school I went to was in the Sinful Bend of Gasconade River. This bend derived its name from plenty of whiskey, big log rollings and dancing parties. The school was taught by Berry Smith in a little log cabin that was built for that purpose. This was in 1850 when I was 12 years of age. Some of my school mates were Silas Moon, Samuel Moon, Benton Elrod, Richard Stotes, John Vaughn and Will Huffman. Among the young ladies who were students in this school were Siana Moon, Mary Ann Stotes and Lucinda Stotes.

I well recollect the first religious services I ever was at . . . The meeting was held at Mr. Billy Scott's. They were the United Baptists, known now as the Missionary Baptists. This was in 1848, when I was six years old. The name of the preacher was Edward Moss and they had communion service and foot washing (in *Turnbo's Tales of the Ozarks*, pp. 24–25).

Great pride is taken in those who settled the Ozarks in the eighteenth and nineteenth centuries. Modern-day hillfolk invariably characterize their ancestors as honest, kind, and good people who were admirable because they were adventurous and independent. Traditional Ozarkers believe they have inherited the worthwhile traits of individualism, self-reliance, and self-sufficiency from those ancestors. They put great stock in being able to handle tasks and chores that others have to hire people to do. In his dissertation, *Autobiography of an American Family*, Donald R. Holliday describes how his own southern Missouri family coped with a large number of essential farm activities:

By accretion, from the time the boys were very young, until they were grown, until they left home, they learned the thousand tricks of shoeing horses and breaking them. They learned how to castrate a calf or a hog without letting either bleed to death. They learned all the details of the eleven-month season of growing tobacco. They learned their father's belief in planting by signs, the hundreds of home remedies for man and animal, and many of the superstitions and potions for counteracting not-quite physical maladies. They all sawed and hammered their way to being fair carpenters, and they mixed mortar and laid rock. Bicycles, plows, tractors, trucks, cars, hayrakes, and mowing machines made mechanics of them, capable, determined, ingenious enough to repair a machine or to get it unstuck and back on the road. Double-bitted axes, cross-cut saw, and mall and wedges made timbermen of them, too (p. 113).

Since most Ozarkers live in rural surroundings, it is hardly surprising that they tend to regard rural life and its values as being superior to what urban life has to offer. This attitude is not unique to Ozarkers but represents a long-standing American tradition of hostility to cities. From at least the time of Thomas Jefferson, many of the country's most distinguished thinkers and writers have viewed the American city as a troubling and troubled place. Thus traditional Ozarkers have as company Henry James, John Dewey, and Theodore Dreiser, among others, when they think of urban areas with distrust, as places of crime and pollution. Nontraditional residents are less likely to regard cities as being populated by immoral and ungodly people.

Certainly, city life and rural life have always been different. Towns were the first to benefit from modern technology and ideas, primarily because of their proximity to modern methods of transportation. Town dwellers were the first to receive modernizing influences such as steam and electric power, newer forms of transportation, improved schools, and social services. Yet these benefits are not as important to traditional

Ozarkers as the individuality and freedom they associate with rural areas. As one person told me, "I'd rather live up here in these old Ozark hills than any place I know. We have it better here than anywhere else."

Traditional families have very sharply defined gender roles. Certain duties, such as cooking (except for fish and wild game), washing dishes, and other household chores are women's work, not to be performed by men. On the other hand, much of what is considered men's work, such as farm chores, is carried out by women as well. This was true in the nineteenth century and applies even more today when women have increasingly taken jobs in factories or stores in order to provide families with a second income.

Although not every Ozark resident attends church, most profess some sort of religious belief. Avowed atheists, usually called infidels by their neighbors, are relatively rare but not unknown. Some years ago one such person held sway in a barber shop, letting everyone know that he regarded Christianity and all other religions as elaborate fictions. The reaction from his captive audience was typical; the discourse didn't endear the man to those waiting for haircuts, but no one tried to prevent him from talking. Most who hold his views are less bold, perhaps choosing caution over candor. Except for those living in certain ethnic communities, traditional Ozarkers hold to fundamentalist religious beliefs and belong to such churches as Church of Christ, Assembly of God, and various Pentecostal churches that feature highly emotional services.

The traditional Ozarker's attitude toward the land is what most vividly separates natives from outsiders. Traditionalists believe that only those born in the Ozarks are capable of making a living from the rugged, often low-quality, soil. They also regard the land as a refuge and a source of important values. Speaking of his own family, Holliday comments: "All of the boys reaped tremendous rewards from the simple fact that they knew, intimately their woods environment. They never questioned the fact, that they could survive in the woods, because they knew well enough the various characteristics of their habitat that they could reap almost anything that nature had to offer. That they knew enough about wild animals, their skill in tracking, hunting, trapping attested. Their knowledge of trees and plants, and their uses, gave them added assurance that nature would support them" (p. 138).

FOLK ARCHITECTURE

At one time the building of homes was essentially a community activity; sometimes people even came from long distances to help in a house-raising. During the first half of the nineteenth century, slaves were sometimes available and did much of the heavy work. In most communities, though, men from the neighborhood performed the arduous task of erecting houses. The most common of the early homes, and probably also the most convenient for pioneers, was the single-room log cabin. Occasionally, it had a porch and a puncheon floor (that is, one made of heavy, broad, roughly dressed timber hewed on one side), but most often there was just a dirt floor. For the building of such houses, very large logs, eighteen or twenty feet long, were obtained from the trunks of oak trees in the nearby forest. Before inviting his neighbors to help, the owner cut the timber and hewed and notched the logs. His friends then lifted the heavy logs into place.

In these early homes, doors and windows were simple, consisting of shutters made with an axe or frow. These heavy, wooden apertures had the virtue of keeping out cold air when closed but the disadvantage of shutting out light unless they were open. Later on, of course, glass was used in windows for most cabins. In *Voices of Moccasin Creek*, Tate Page, who grew up in the southern Ozarks of Arkansas in the second decade of the twentieth century, describes the glass window in his family's cabin and its effect on lighting:

Single-pen log cabin, Taney County, Missouri, ca. 1840 (Photo courtesy James M. Denny, Missouri Department of Natural Resources)

Only one four-pane glass window gave outside light to the living room area of the original cabin. The opening had been made by removing sections of two of the logs of the wall north of the fireplace and boxing the hole in with suitable sections of rough plank. The window did not open, and lighted only the nearby portion of the room. In the winter, at night, a roaring fire lighted and heated the room. A coaloil lamp or lantern was sometimes used for additional light. The lamp was used occasionally for light at night in the summer, but it attracted so many flying and creeping things that its use was usually avoided. The unscreened front entrance, when the door was open, provided some light on summer days, but the interior, at best, was badly lighted (p. 26).

Until the second quarter of the twentieth century, log cabin roofs were commonly covered with clapboards, generally cut in lengths of two, three, or four feet. If nails were available, clapboards were nailed to laths split from smaller timbers and then to rafters for support. In the nineteenth century, nails often were unavailable, in which case clapboards were fastened to the roof by weight poles laid on the boards and secured by intertwining withes around the ends to hold them in place. As the need for additional space arose, lean-to kitchens were frequently added to the backs of the single-room log cabins.

Eventually, the single-pen log cabin was supplanted by a larger type of log cabin consisting of two large rooms with a central hallway and often a porch as well. The origins of these and of other log cabin construction techniques have long been a matter of debate among scholars. In an in-

Nathan Boone House, Greene County, Missouri, ca. 1837, central-passage log (Photo courtesy James M. Denny, Missouri Department of Natural Resources)

fluential book, *The Log Cabin Myth* (1939), Harold R. Shurtleff argued for a Swedish origin. Shurtleff's thesis was bolstered by the undeniable fact that the seventeenth-century settlers of New Sweden were the first to make extensive use of log construction. Even so, Fred Kniffen and Henry Glassie challenged Shurtleff's conclusion, noting that Swedes were unlikely to have transferred log building technology to the greater population because there were so few of them. Kniffen and Glassie maintain that eighteenth-century German migrants should be credited with introducing log cabin construction techniques to the New World. More recently, Terry G. Jordan, basing his conclusions on extensive fieldwork in Europe, has challenged Kniffen and Glassie, maintaining that Swedes were indeed responsible for introducing the technique in North America. Regardless of where the technology originated, early Ozark settlers made use of the knowledge in building their homes.

The inside of the cabin was decorated with paper, a new layer usually being added every year. Tate Page gives a good account of the method and its effect:

The papering was fantastic in its variety of print types, content, and art work. Attractive selections from magazines that had come into possession of the family were there to be seen by one and all. Some of the space was covered with bright-colored pages from the Sears Roebuck catalogue, and from other sources that appealed to the lady of the house. All paper was hoarded carefully as it was unbelievably scarce. The best was selected for "papering" the walls. The pictures and

Louis Bolduc House, Ste. Genevieve, Missouri, ca. late eighteenth century *poteaux sur solle* (Photocopied from photo by Jack E. Boucher, Historic American Buildings Survey [HABS])

Guibord-Valle House, Ste. Genevieve, Missouri, ca. 1806, *poteaux sur solle* (Photocopied from photo by Jack E. Boucher, HABS)

the "part-stories" were a source of endless pleasure on a rainy day. By moving the lamp or carrying a lighted pine splinter around the room the beholder could travel in dreams beyond the mountains to another world. No story was ever complete. The end, the middle, or the beginning had to be filled in by the imagination of the reader or its incompleteness ignored (in *Voices of Moccasin Creek*, p. 27).

Amoreaux House, Ste. Genevieve, Missouri, ca. late eighteenth century, *poteaux en terre* (Photocopied from photo by Jack E. Boucher, HABS)

Of course, not all the houses built in the Ozarks during the nineteenth and early twentieth centuries were log cabins; many were of frame construction. Frame houses were of two basic types: those built by British-American techniques of braced, balloon, and box frames and those involving *poteaux en terre* (upright posts anchored in the ground) and *poteaux sur solle* (upright posts resting on a wooden sill and a masonry foundation). The latter generally was found in the northeastern Ozarks in regions where the French settled in the eighteenth and nineteenth centuries, but there are some exceptions to this rule. For example, a house in Independence County, Arkansas, in the southern Ozarks is made of *poteaux en terre* construction. This anomaly is explained by the fact that the house was built by black slaves who moved to the Ozarks from Louisiana.

The first frame buildings in the Ozarks were of braced frame construction, but after the Civil War this technique was generally abandoned, except in the building of barns. In this type of structure, which derived from medieval European building technology, heavy, hand-hewn upright posts, measuring four inches wide by up to ten inches thick, were placed at corners and intermediate spaces to hold up window and door openings. Studs, generally measuring two inches by four inches, were used for support between the posts. Posts and studs were tied together with sills at the bottom and plates at the top. Diagonal braces extending from the posts down to the sills gave added stability to the corner posts. Mortise and tenon joints or nails were used to join framing members. Vertical

Sherrill-Hoff House, Stockton, Cedar County, Missouri, ca. 1850s. (Photo courtesy James M. Denny, Missouri Department of Natural Resources)

Grey-Campbell house, Springfield, Greene County, Missouri, ca. 1850s. Bottom courses of siding are gone revealing braced frame (Photo courtesy James M. Denny, Missouri Department of Natural Resources)

boards or lath and plaster sealed the interior, and horizontal weatherboards generally covered the exterior.

In the late nineteenth century, braced-frame structures were generally replaced by balloon framing. Having originated about three decades before the Civil War, this technique was essentially an updating of brace framing. By the 1870s standardized lumber and inexpensive wire nails were readily available, a beneficial situation for those wanting to use this method. In balloon framing, walls were composed entirely of lightweight two-by-four-inch studs attached to sills and plates by nails that were stabilized by interior and exterior sheathing. This construction technique is the one found most often in the Ozarks after about 1870.

One other type of frame construction was used frequently from about 1870 to about 1920. This was box framing and consisted of vertical boards, ranging from six to twelve inches wide and generally no more than one inch thick, nailed to sills and plates. These vertical boards not only provided major structural support but also served as both interior and exterior wall. Window and door casings protruded into the building's rooms. Frequently, windows and doors were flanked by supporting two-by-four-inch studs. Board-and-batten siding made of wood strips covered the cracks between the vertical boards. About 1910 many buildings added horizontal weatherboards to the exterior, thereby making these houses appear to be the same as braced or balloon-frame houses. For several years box framing was considered a desirable, economical alternative to other

Detail of balloon framing, Westphalia, Osage County, Missouri, post-Civil War (Photo courtesy Lynn Morrow)

Saddle-bag, box frame house, Taney County, Missouri (Photo courtesy Lynn Morrow)

framing methods and an improvement over the log cabin. Consequently, many people replaced their log homes with box-frame houses.

The typical house in the Ozarks in the nineteenth century was relatively small and generally of one story, although many homes had a loft that was used either as a place for sleeping or for storage. There were, however, some larger houses; in the antebellum years one type was the I-house, which was a two-story building of one room in depth. As it did elsewhere, the I-house symbolized economic achievement in the Ozarks.

In the last two decades of the nineteenth century, Ozark residents, like those in many other parts of the country, started using some architectural ideas found in midcentury pattern books. These volumes represented a change in approaches to building. Previously, the architectural ideal was balance based on symmetry, but in the pattern books, which were originally intended to appeal to the middle class, the ideal was balance based upon an organic asymmetry. This mode facilitated the incorporation of new spaces within the home, and the pattern books suggested new methods of incorporating spaces previously enclosed in rear shed or

I-house, Cedar County, Missouri, ca. 1850s (Photo courtesy James M. Denny, Missouri Department of Natural Resources)

I-house, Iron County, Missouri, ca. 1820s (Photo courtesy James M. Denny, Missouri Department of Natural Resources)

ell additions. This led to the development of "bent" or "prow" houses, the latter a colloquial term used because the house's central projection resembled the prow of a ship.

These prow houses, consisting of gabled projections centered on the front facade, quickly became a status symbol. Sarah Brown's remarks about the prow house as found in a single state could apply to the entire Ozarks: "The rise of these bent houses . . . has been associated with a shift from subsistence and general farming, which entailed the growing of some wheat and cotton for cash, to the specialized farming of fruit such as apples, strawberries, and grapes. Even for the more well-to-do of these farmers, the bent house reflected a minimum of change of traditional forms. Prow houses are, in fact, double-pen houses with front extensions. The two-story prow house fills the same socioeconomic slot as the I-house and somewhat replaces it in the landscape" (in *An Arkansas Folklore Sourcebook*, p. 124).

The last major development in Ozark folk architecture came about the time of World War Two. This was the arrival of the bungalow, a form

I-house, probably balloon frame, ca. late nineteenth century (Photo courtesy Lynn Morrow)

that had been all the rage among early-twentieth-century middle-class American house builders. The term "bungalow," according to Clay Lancaster, is "less a descriptive label than an impressionistic qualitative concept that could be applied to a diverse, apparently dissimilar group of dwellings" (in *Common Places*, p. 79). Some bungalows were quite elaborate, while others were relatively small. It was the smaller ones that were usually built in the Ozarks.

Brick was used for some houses but was more popular for wells, spring-houses, and other outbuildings and for the foundations and chimneys of both wood and log houses. Chimneys, of course, were also made of stone, both mortared and unmortared. The Shannon Cabin, built in 1902 about six miles from Mountain View, Arkansas, removed in 1986, and rebuilt at the Ozark Folk Center, had an unmortared stone chimney. Stone was not a popular building material for dwellings in most sections of the Ozarks but was frequently used for commercial buildings such as grocery stores.

Bungalows in Thayer, Oregon County, Missouri (Photo courtesy Lynn Morrow)

FURNITURE MAKING

During the early nineteenth century, most dwellers in the Ozarks had to make their own furniture. In many communities there was simply no ready-made furniture available for purchase. There were, however, trees in abundance in most sections of the Ozarks, so it was common for home owners to make bedsteads, tables, chairs, chests of drawers, and whatever else was needed. Initially, the lack of necessary tools meant that the furniture was crude, but as such implements became available, some men showed a real talent for this sort of work. By 1870 a large number of furniture makers were active in the Ozark region. Earlier than that, in some urban centers, merchants had been importing furniture from eastern factories. For example, in 1834 Fort Smith businessman J. Bigelow advertised in the *Arkansas Gazette* that he had received "a large fresh supply of GROCERIES—Cognac, Brandy, Holland Gin, Jamaica Rum, Rye

Bungalow, Taney
County, Missouri (Photo
courtesy Lynn Morrow)

Whiskey, Madiera . . . also FURNITURE, consisting of bedsteads, bu-
reaus, tables, etc." (in *Arkansas Made*, vol. 1, p. 13).

However, throughout the nineteenth and the first quarter of the twentieth centuries, rural residents of the Ozarks usually got their furniture
from local craftsmen or made their own. In general, simplicity and durability were the keynotes when it came to providing home furnishings.
Most often furniture was made of cedar, cherry, white oak, ash, hickory,
maple, or walnut, all woods that were available nearby and that would last
a long time.

Chairs were among the most important items of furniture in the home.
It was not uncommon for a chair to last for fifty years or more. In 1929
one craftsman described how such sturdy chairs were made:

My first chair-making was when I was 16 years old and I still enjoy making them.
I have made a many one in the 60 years' time. The wood used is ash, white oak,
and hickory. My first work was done with a foot-power lathe; then for a time I
used the modern-type engine for power; but today I have dropped back to the old
method of using a drawing knife, some broken glass, a piece of sand paper, and
my pocket knife.

The rounds are made first and are made from hickory and oak. These are
thoroughly dried. Sometimes through the winter season enough rounds for about
40 chairs are made and by spring they are well seasoned. If I am in a hurry to
make a set of chairs, the rounds are put into the bake oven of the cookstove after
the meal has been cooked, and in a few days' time this way one can thoroughly
dry out enough rounds for a set of chairs.

The posts are cut, when the rounds are dry, and finished as fast as possible so
as to use them while they are very green. The holes are bored in them and the
seasoned rounds set in and driven down with a two-pound hammer. The slats for
the back-boards have to be made before the posts, because they have to be crimped
by putting them in a press. By the time the posts are made the back-boards are

pretty well crimped and all parts are ready to assemble. The shrinking of the post around the seasoned rounds holds them firm. Wooden pegs are often driven in to hold the rounds fast—but never a nail.

The bottom is the last part finished. It is made of hickory bark, or white oak splints (in *A Study of the Home and Local Crafts of the Pioneers of Washington County, Arkansas*).

There are still craftsmen who adhere to the old-fashioned method of chairmaking described here, but most of those active in the Ozarks today use modern power equipment.

Other forms of furniture locally made during the nineteenth century included bedsteads, tables, cabinets, dressers, wardrobes, bookcases, cedar chests, and picture frames. Many of these items were built by craftsmen for their own homes, but the making of cabinets, bedsteads, tables, and dressers soon evolved into a small local industry. By 1870 the more populous Ozark counties, such as Washington County, Arkansas, had strong cabinetmaking traditions. Many of these local crafts industries continue to the present.

LIGHTING

Except in the cases of those few people deliberately seeking a return to a simpler life-style, such as the Amish and some back-to-the-landers, homes today have electric lighting. Before this modern convenience became available—in some sections of the Ozarks that wasn't until World War Two—three other types of lighting were used. The most primitive of these was the grease lamp, which was exactly what its name implies—lighting derived from grease. Grease and a strip of twisted cotton were put into a tin box, or some similar container, and when the cotton was saturated, one end was pushed through a hole cut in the lid of the box and lighted. This gave off a rather meager light and, according to some people, an unpleasant odor as well. Although such lights were used well into the twentieth century by some families, most people chose to use dipped candles. Towns of any size generally had a chandlery, but in most households someone, generally the women, were capable of making plain candles. A piece of twisted-yarn thread, six to eight inches in length, was dipped into tallow taken from the renderings after a calf was butchered. The string was first dipped into melted tallow, then held in the air above the vessel until the tallow on the thread hardened. It was repeatedly dipped and cooled again until enough tallow adhered to the string to form a candle. The finished product was then heated slightly on one end and set on a pasteboard base. The process of making candles got easier when

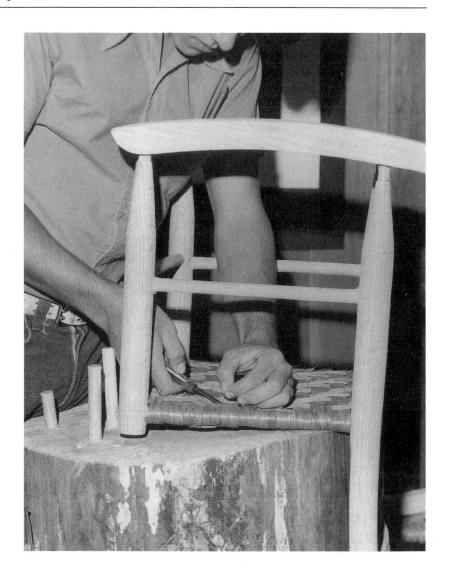

Modern-day furniture maker completing a chair in the old-fashioned style (Photo courtesy Ozark Folk Center)

candle molds became commonplace in the region. In some communities the first person to purchase a mold loaned it to many of his neighbors who, seeing the utensil's usefulness, then purchased one for his household. This "chain marketing" resulted in more efficient candlemaking.

Candles were replaced by kerosene lamps, which in turn were supplanted by electric lights. This change from one form of lighting to another occurred rather rapidly, as is attested to by one Arkansas woman who wrote radio entertainer F. S. Bauersfeld in the late 1930s, "I am sixty-six years old and have seen four kinds of light—grease light, candle light, kerosene lamps and electric light" (in *Tales of the Early Days*, p. 138).

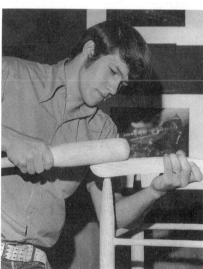

Candles and candleholders made out of native wood (Photo courtesy *The Ozarks Mountaineer*)

CLOTHING AND OTHER DOMESTIC CRAFTS

In the nineteenth and early twentieth centuries Ozark residents typically had small wardrobes—usually three sets of clothing, of which two were for daily wear and one was for Sunday. There were many reasons for this sparse selection of clothes. For the most part, homes were small and had no closets, so there was simply no space available. Also, making clothing was very time consuming, and housewives had many other arduous tasks. And some families were simply too poor to afford much in the way of clothing, even when it was homemade.

Producing clothing required the making of machinery such as flax wheels, cracking-reels, spinning wheels, and looms. Flax wheels were used to spin material for finer articles of clothing, whereas the spinning wheel was used to provide thread for everything else. A century ago most farms grew flax that was cut in the fall, tied in bundles, and then scattered on the ground to undergo a process called "dew-rotting," which aided in breaking down the woody stalk covering, a process that took three or four weeks. It was then gathered up, broken, and hackled. The hackle consisted of numerous small iron spindles firmly fastened into a board or heavy block of wood. Flax fibers were combed through these sharpened spindles until they were made ready for spinning.

Wool and cotton were the other raw materials used in making clothing in nineteenth-century Ozark homes; most farms grew cotton and had some sheep. Both wool and cotton required laborious processing. After wool had been sheared from the sheep, it had to be burred—i.e., the burs were removed—washed, and broken before it was finally carded into rolls. Cotton gathered from plants in the field had to be separated from the seeds. In a few areas of the Ozarks, cotton gins were available for this separation of fibers from the seeds. In most areas, however, cotton was not grown in sufficient quantity to warrant gins, so the process of "finger picking" was used. In the 1920s two ladies described this method in detail: "We usually finger picked the cotton . . . after supper was over and the younger children had been put to bed. The older members of the family helped and, as a rule, enough cotton was separated in one night to keep the mother busy carding and spinning the next day; or else enough to pad a quilt, depending upon which of these articles was most needed" (in *A Study of the Home and Local Crafts of the Pioneers of Washington County, Arkansas*, p. 27).

The development of hand-powered cotton gins facilitated this process. Two persons who sat facing each other operated these gins by turning a crank on each end of two round steel rods that were fastened closely together. One person fed the cotton while the other removed lint, and the seeds dropped down. Carding was the final step before the spinning of both cotton and wool. This chore was usually done at night before bed. Some women were not skilled at carding wool and cotton into rolls, so those adept at the craft frequently performed it for their neighbors.

Once carding was completed, spinning was the final process before the transforming of flax, cotton, or wool into clothing. In the nineteenth century, flax and spinning wheels were commonly found in Ozark homes. By the first decade of the twentieth century, both were rapidly falling out of favor, and two elderly, very traditional, gentlemen in Wideman, Arkansas, commented that in the late 1920s they did not recall seeing but one spinning wheel in any of the homes in their neighborhood, even though they lived in a rural community where one might expect to find such equipment at that time. The spinning wheel used throughout the nineteenth century was a variation on the so-called great wheel that was known in Europe as early as the fourteenth century.

Knitting was an important skill for nineteenth-century housewives because it was the means of providing socks and laces for the family. Until the availability of commercially made lighting accessories, housewives also typically knitted lamp wicks. Knitting had to be done after the other housework was completed, which usually meant in the evening. Even the most proficient knitters couldn't turn out a great quantity in a short time. Each family member had to have at least four pairs of socks, and anyone producing one pair a day was considered to have done a "pretty good day's work." Although highly skilled knitters can still be found, it is an activity no longer done out of necessity. As one woman said, "I like to knit because it gives me a lot of pleasure."

Knitting needles were also used in making lace, a luxury item that was used to dress up otherwise drab-looking articles, including homespun sheets and pillowcases. Other forms of decorative trimming, such as handmade fringe, were often used to make items more esthetically pleasing.

Weaving was an especially important skill for early housewives, since all cloth and clothing were the product of the loom. Essential woven items included bed ticks, mattress covers, table linens, towels, blankets, sheets, pillow cases, coverlets, floor coverings, and counterpanes. Production of these articles was extremely time consuming; the completion of three yards of material was considered a very good day's work. Until the 1870s the chief bed covers were coverlets and blankets, not because quilting was unknown, but because in typical Ozark households cloth scraps used in making quilts were relatively scarce. Coverlet weaving is still practiced, although as is the case with many other pioneer crafts, it is no longer done from necessity.

Floor coverings were far more important in the nineteenth and early twentieth centuries than they are today because they were used on every square inch of the floor. One Washington County, Arkansas, resident recalled: "I remember our old log house with its puncheon floor, and the yards and yards of carpet it took to cover the floor. There were forty yards

Dorothy Ford, Pleasant Grove, Arkansas, working at the weaving loom (Photo courtesy Ozark Folk Center)

in one room" (in *A Study of the Home and Local Crafts of the Pioneers of Washington County, Arkansas*, pp. 34–35). There were several reasons for this custom. One undoubtedly was that people just considered these coverings esthetically pleasing. But more practical considerations were that the coverings helped keep houses warmer in winter and cooler in summer and that they discouraged visits from mice, rats, and snakes.

Before cloth was woven, it was often dyed. This was done primarily for esthetic reasons; people simply wanted to make their fabrics more colorful. Women went into the woods to gather plants such as sumac, green cedar, and the indigo bush and barks such as walnut and hickory and converted them into dyes of varied colors. Walnut hulls were used for black and brown, sassafras roots for red, hickory bark for yellow, and indigo for blue. In the nineteenth century, indigo was very popular, in part because of its ability to last a long time without fading. In the late 1920s, when Bonita Musgrave conducted her study of pioneer crafts in Washington County, Arkansas, she examined a number of items that retained their colors even though they had been dyed seventy or eighty years earlier.

Sewing and needlework were also important skills in earlier times and are still commonly practiced today. In most nineteenth-century Ozark households, sewing was, of necessity, done by hand, and even in the present day many women prefer to do without sewing machines when it comes to their most important sewing.

Of the numerous traditional skills performed by pioneer Ozark women none has a more vital life today than quilting. This craft can easily be traced back four centuries and is probably even older. For a variety of reasons, of which the most important was the availability of quilts from other sources such as mail order houses, quilting underwent a relative decline in popularity from about 1880 to about 1925; however, even during those years it could not really have been called a dying craft. In recent years the emergence of statewide, regional, and even national quilting societies that hold frequent meetings and generally encourage quilting has insured that the craft is not likely to disappear anytime soon. These societies have also spawned a phenomenon that was previously unknown: quilts produced as art objects. Such quilts are intended mainly for gallery walls, and some quilters are greatly offended by the suggestion that their work should be used solely as bed coverings.

Doing research in the Ozarks during the 1930s, Vance Randolph and Isabel Spradley discovered how popular quilting was. In a small area of southwest Missouri and northwest Arkansas, they collected 438 names for quilt patterns. Although little detail is provided about how the informants learned these names, it seems likely that at least some were from newspapers and magazines that frequently printed quilt patterns. Many of these

Lois Dodson, Mountain
View, Arkansas, working
on a quilt (Photo courtesy
The Ozark Folk Center)

magazines, such as *Grit*, were primarily sold in rural areas of the United States. Such sources, though, were certainly not the only influences on Ozark quilters; many had their information from oral tradition.

Quilting in the Ozarks has long been a social occasion exclusively for women. A typical nineteenth-century quilting was described by Fanny Love, a Van Buren County, Arkansas, resident, in her diary entry for December 12, 1861: "Mrs. Garner asked us to a quilting this evening . . . I went down to Mrs. Garners this morning we like to froze . . . When we got there I found all the girls. There was twenty four of us and not the first boy, never saw girls enjoy themselves better in my life. . . . We quilted all day, but did not get the quilt rolled finished and taken off the frame, it was quilted in flowers" (in *Arkansas Made*, vol. 1, p. 85).

At one time a number of customs were considered essential before a newly completed quilt could be "christened." Vance Randolph describes some of the more common of these traditions: "Groups of unmarried women at quilting bees used to shake up a cat in the newly completed quilt and then stand around in a big circle as the animal was suddenly released. The theory was that the girl toward whom the cat jumped would be the first of the company to catch a husband. At other times the quilters would wrap an engaged girl up in the new quilt and roll her under the bed, but the exact significance of this procedure has never been explained to me" (in *Ozark Magic and Folklore*, p. 185).

Piecing, or pieced work, was the most popular quilting technique in the Ozarks during the nineteenth century and remains so to the present day. This technique involves taking numerous pieces of geometrically cut decorative fabrics and sewing them together, edge to edge, to create a block or repeat design that becomes the quilt top. Generally, piecing consists of very tiny, almost invisible stitches, but some quilters make much larger, more visible stitches. Those who take this easier path are generally considered poor quilters.

Other less popular techniques are appliqué and stuffed work. Appliqué, a French term meaning "to lay on," consists of stitching small pieces of fabric that are sewn together to create a specific motif onto a larger background piece. The background fabric serves, in effect, as the quilt's front when the top, filling, and backing are sewn together. Stuffed work is used either separately or in combination with piecing of appliqué. Normally quilts are stuffed after the quilting is completed. The woven threads of the backing are separated by needle, with pieces of cotton batting then being carefully forced through the openings until the desired padded effect is achieved. Then the hole is closed by realigning the separate warp and weft threads. Both appliqué and stuffed work are more popular than ever before, but even now they are not as common in the Ozarks as piecing.

It would be impossible to list all the quilt patterns that are popular in the Ozarks. In 1942 Marguerite Lyon wrote that the Double Wedding Ring and China Platter were the favorite patterns, but she also cited the Stamp, the Cobblestone, the Wild Goose Chase, the Tulip, the Lone Star, and the Magnolia Bud as being frequently chosen. Perhaps those were the favorites in the Missouri Ozarks where Lyon lived but, even in the 1940s, a larger number of patterns had some popularity, including Star of Bethlehem, Irish Chain, Rocky Mountain Road, Peony, Rattlesnake, Feathered Star, Ocean Waves, Rose of Sharon, Whigs' Defeat, and Oak Leaf and Reel. There are no patterns unique to the Ozarks; all of those reported to date are regional variations, sometimes with different names, of patterns known more widely.

Quilting, especially for traditional quilters, is, and apparently has long been, mainly a spare-time activity. Nevertheless, it is an important one for women, and many probably agree with Almeda Riddle, who once said, "I just enjoy quilting, it relaxes me about as much as anything. That's why I like to do it." A few traditional quilters, seeing it as more than just an enjoyable activity, but as a means of additional income, have established shops where they sell handmade quilts.

One traditional clothing craft that was commonplace in the nine-teenth-century Ozarks—shoemaking—has entirely disappeared. Al-though shoes were a necessity, at no time were there more than a few people skilled at this work, and they were kept very busy, especially dur-ing the winter months, since in warm weather children usually went bare-footed. A good shoemaker could produce a pair of shoes per day, once the leather was processed. Maple wood was used to fashion lasts on which shoes were made. Wooden pegs fastened together the upper parts and soles of shoes.

Boots took a longer time to make than shoes, with a good craftsman producing a pair in three days. The upper portion of the leather was crimped by a board of much the same shape as the foot and instep, and leather was stretched over this until it was the proper shape. The main tools used in shoemaking were a broadfaced hammer and a shoe knife, instruments that were hand-forged in the blacksmith shop.

FOODWAYS

Many songs, of which the best known is probably "The State of Arkan-sas," comment on the scarcity of food in the nineteenth-century Ozarks. While these ballads are intended to be humorous, the dilemma was a real one; having sufficient food was a daily concern in most rural areas. Sev-eral crafts, the most important being milling, were developed to help solve the problem. Corn was the favorite food crop in the pioneer Ozarks and remains so today. Wheat was also grown on farms, and both wheat and corn had to be ground into flour and meal before they could be used in making breads. Traditionally, neighbors pitched in to help process crops. Indeed, at one time such activities as corn shuckings were regarded as major social events in rural Ozark communities. Silas Turnbo collected the following account of one old-time corn shucking in Arkansas from a Mr. Fie Snow:

I got permission to remain overnight at a Mr. Jones' who before nightfall told me that there would be a big corn shucking there that night on the Tennessee style. Jones had 1,500 bushels of corn heaped up in the lot near his barn. By this time, the weather was clear and warm and most of the snow had melted, but the corn was yet covered with snow. Before night set in, young men and old men began to assemble until near sixty had collected at the pile of corn and we all went to work with yarn gloves on and had a fine time that night shucking corn and putting it in the barn and rolling the shucks back out of the way. We never stopped until we had finished the corn, but it took us until just before daybreak to get it done.

Then to rest ourselves, we all wrestled together and ran and jumped until day light. After day light, we got into a game of "jumping over big toe" which is done by taking hold of your big toe with one hand and jumping the other foot over it. In carrying out the game, you must hold your right toe with your left hand and jump your left foot over it, or you can reverse it and jump your right foot over it. This sort of maneuver is hard to do and there were only a few that were able to perform it. The play looked impossible to do to one young fellow. After I had proposed to carry it out successful, he offered to put up a nice little mare and a good saddle and bridle for that day and time against its equal value that I could not do it. As I did not have enough money to put up against his mare and equipment, I refused to bet with him, but I showed him that I could. Of course I could not go through with it without falling down, and this ended it. The woman had cooked nearly all night and we ate a fine breakfast that morning and bidding my new friends adieu, I went on my way and arrived at my destination in a few days more (in *Turnbo's Tales*, pp. 89–90).

Harvesting of wheat was done by cradling. The hands began work in the ripest field, then went to the next ripest crop, proceeding until every field of wheat was harvested. Threshing of wheat was done by hand with a flail or by treading, i. e., driving horses over the wheat to break the grain loose from the husks and chaff. This was followed by winnowing, the separation of chaff from the grain either by use of the wind or a hat.

After harvesting and other necessary processes were completed, both wheat and corn were taken to the mill, where for a percentage of the product a farmer was able to have his crops converted into flour and meal. These trips to the mill were rare in pioneer days, typically occurring about twice a year, since there were few mills in most counties and roads were often poor and rough. Perhaps because they took a percentage of the product in exchange for their work, millers traditionally were considered dishonest and unscrupulous. A widely known song still performed today called "The Miller's Will" graphically conveys the regard in which millers were held. The following version was collected by Vance Randolph from Dr. George E. Hastings, in Fayetteville, Arkansas, in 1938:

> There was an old miller an' he lived all alone,
> He had three sons an' they was grown,
> An' when he went to make his will,
> All that he had was a little old mill,
> To my whack fol doodle day,
> To my whack fol doodle day.
>
> He called to him his oldest son,
> Says my course is almost run,
> An' if you the miller I should make,
> How much toll are you goin' for to take?

To my whack fol doodle day,
To my whack fol doodle day.

The boy says father, my name is Jake,
An' out of each bushel I'll take a peck,
Of every bushel that I do grind,
I hope by that a good living to find.
To my whack fol doodle day,
To my whack fol doodle day!

He called to him his second son,
Says my course is almost run,
An' if you the miller I should make,
How much toll are you goin' for to take?
To my whack fol doodle day,
To my whack fol doodle day!

The boy says father, my name is Ralph,
An' out of each bushel I'll take a half,
Of every bushel that I do grind,
I hope by that a good living to find.
To my whack fol doodle day,
To my whack fol doodle day!

He called to him his youngest son,
Says my course is almost run,
An' if you the miller I should make,
How much toll are you goin' for to take?
To my whack fol doodle day,
To my whack fol doodle day!

The boy says father, I'm your son,
An' out of four pecks I'll leave but one,
An' if by that a good living I lack,
I'll take all the corn an' swear to the sack!
To my whack fol doodle day,
To my whack fol doodle day!

Although it does not occur in this version, usually the youngest son, that is, the one who cheats his customers out of the most product, is given the mill.

Peas were an especially important part of the winter diet on Ozark farms, and almost every farmer had a pea patch. Fall was the time for picking peas, which was generally, but not exclusively, done by women and children. Once the pods were picked, they were dumped onto a sheet spread on the ground in the yard. Pods were then pounded or thrashed with a stick until all the shells were empty. Then the peas were scooped up and placed in containers. Once the containers were full, peas were then poured back onto the sheet for winnowing. When the peas were clean they were placed in containers in an effort to keep them safe from various insects, rats, and mice.

Storage of food was a continuing problem in pioneer homes, and a number of techniques were devised that are no longer used. One was the pounding of flour into a barrel with a wooden maul, which was done to keep worms and weevils from getting into the flour. The more tightly it was packed, the safer it was from insects. Another solution to the storage problem was the drying of fruits and vegetables, such as peaches, peas, apples, corn, and pumpkin. At a later date, canning was widely practiced, but in the early nineteenth century it was unknown. The technique of drying various fruits and vegetables was explained in 1929 by an eighty-two-year-old resident of Washington County, Arkansas:

The first drying was done on scaffolds in the sun. The fruit was peeled and quartered and spread out on the scaffold. It required much labor to cut and dry thirty or forty bushels of fresh apples. Often it would rain and we always had to bring it in at night to keep it from turning dark. Three or four days of hot sunshine, though, and a batch was ready to sack and then it was less trouble to handle. It could be dried in the sacks from then on.

Corn wasn't so much trouble to dry. The ears were gathered while in the stage for roasting-ears, and the grains were cut from the cob and placed on a sheet or something and put on the scaffold to dry much the same as apples.

Dried pumpkin, for those golden pies, was considered a table delicacy which no housewife could get along without. These pumpkins were usually dried in the house on a pole or an old quilting frame, put up for this purpose, near the kitchen stove or fire place. Strips of beautiful golden pumpkin were hung over these poles, and the heat from the fire soon dried them out until they could be sacked for later use.

When it was an unusually rainy season, we used to build kilns, for drying purposes, out under a shed some place. The kiln was built of stones, with large, flat rocks, on top, and a fire was built beneath it to form heat for the drying of the fruit, which was placed on the rocks. Both methods of drying fruit were quite a job but my! my! we enjoyed working then—because we always dried enough fruit and vegetables for home use, and sold several bushels of dried apples at one dollar per bushel; that's the way we bought our Sunday dresses sixty years ago, which were nothing more than calico (in *A Study of the Home and Local Crafts of the Pioneers of Washington County, Arkansas*, pp. 47–48).

In many sections of the Ozarks, especially in northwest Arkansas, apples were plentiful and were used in the making of apple butter, one of the few table delicacies to be found in most homes during the pioneer era.

Making apple butter required a great deal of work. First, apples were placed in a press and crushed to make cider. Then apples and sugar, in equal proportions, were put in a large kettle or pan, and cider was poured over the mixture until the vessel was almost full. This concoction was cooked for a long time over very low heat until it was the right consistency for spreading on a piece of bread. Stone jars were used to store the apple butter that couldn't be used immediately.

Maple syrup and maple sugar were other delicacies found in nineteenth-century Ozark homes. The techniques used in producing these forms of sweetening are described as follows: "Sugar maples are native trees of the forests in this section, and, as a rule, one man tapped thirty to forty trees. This was done by boring holes in the trees and placing splitcane troughs into these for the sap or juice to escape, which was caught in pails. This was then put into the old-fashioned wash kettle and cooked until it was thick as desired for syrup. If maple sugar was desired, it was cooked until thick like candy, then poured into pans or molds and cut into shape when cool. Mothers of the forties and fifties took much pride in making such specialties" (in *A Study of the Home and Local Crafts of the Pioneers of Washington County, Arkansas*, pp. 51–52).

An even more important type of sweetening was molasses, which caught on quickly in the Ozarks after sorghum grain was introduced in the 1850s. Silas Turnbo describes how sorghum first came to his section of the Missouri Ozarks:

I remember distinctly when the seed of sorghum cane was first introduced into our neighborhood when we lived on the farm on the south bank of White River in the southeast corner of Taney County, Missouri. In the fall of 1857, my father went on a visit to Decatur and Maury Counties, Tennessee, to see his relatives and brought a few of the seed with him to Taney County. Later on in the fall of the same year, John Jones moved here from Tennessee and he brought a few of the seed with him. The seed had been introduced in some localities in Tennessee in the early spring of 1857.

My father had just enough seed to plant nine short rows in a small patch of land on the bank of the river just below a little hollow. The sorghum was planted between the river bank and the graveyard and was just over the line in Ozark County, Missouri. Of course, the seed was not planted until the spring of 1858, and when it had matured in August, our first start at making syrup was ludicrous. After stripping the blades from the stocks and cutting down the stocks and taking them where we wanted to make the syrup, we cut the stocks into small bits and placed them into a trough and mashed them with a billet like Indians beating corn. We now put the stuff in a pot and poured water in. We boiled the juice out and reduced it to a syrup and strained it through a coarse cloth. It did not take

Sorghum making in the Ozarks (Photo courtesy *The Ozarks Mountaineer*)

long to find out that this process of making molasses was a failure and other means had to be resorted to.

My father now hired John Anderson to make two wooden rollers to press the juice from the cane. Anderson tried to make them with drawer knife and ax but they failed to work and then my father hired Martin Johnson to make a sorghum mill of wood and he succeeded in doing it and the cane was run through it and the juice squeezed out. This mill was the first of the kind made on this part of White River. The cane juice was reduced to a syrup by boiling it in iron kettles. No one understood then how to make molasses without scorching them and they were as black as tar or stone coal which colored the lips and gums and teeth a deep black (in *Turnbo's Tales*, p. 152).

Although few accounts like this exist, it is likely that sorghum was introduced to other sections of the Ozarks in a similar fashion.

Molasses making usually takes place in September. To ensure the best quality syrup, the farmer has to cut the cane when it is at the appropriate stage of ripeness and before it is affected by frost. Wooden paddles especially made for the purpose are used to strip the outer leaves of the stalks. Cane is then stacked, loaded on wagons, and carried to the mill where it is converted into syrup. Mules, confined to a long pole called a sweep, operate the press by walking endlessly around the press. There are three essential tasks involved in producing sorghum molasses: "feeding," or pushing the stalks through the roller of the press, tending the fire, and watching the cooking pan. Although traditionally mules were always used, now they are sometimes replaced by a tractor or some kind of motor. Otherwise, molasses making is still done the way it has been for generations.

The cooking equipment consists of a wood-burning furnace topped by a long, flat copper cooking pan constructed with a number of baffles through which the syrup passes in the cooking process. The fire tender is very important to the whole procedure, because he or she determines the color, taste, and consistency of the molasses. If the fire gets too hot the molasses will be scorched, and if it doesn't get hot enough the syrup will be too strong and dark. Once the syrup achieves the correct color and consistency, it is forced out of the spout at the end of the cooking pan into cans, jars, or barrels. Every able-bodied family member helps with molasses making, which is quite unpleasant because September in the Ozarks is usually warm and muggy. Moreover, the cane plant frequently cuts fingers and arms and irritates the skin. This is probably the reason why so few people make molasses today; those who do, however, have no difficulty in selling their product.

Several years ago an elderly resident of the Arkansas Ozarks described how families once acquired their annual meat supply:

There was a time when wild game, such as deer and turkey, were plentiful within the county; yet no family depended upon such a source for the yearly supply of meat. Occasionally this kind of game was killed, but, as a rule, all the neighbors shared in the feast at such time, and no means of curing or trying to keep such meat were practiced. *They just all got together and had a good time.*

The main source of meat was through the butchering of hogs raised on the farm and in the range. Usually from ten to fifteen hogs were butchered each year. All efforts were made to save the lard and cracklings, in fact, *there was no waste.* After butchering and dressing the hogs, the meat was put down in salt in a large box in the old smoke house made for this purpose. As a rule, after it had been in salt from three to six weeks, it was taken out of the salt, washed and hung on poles swung from the joists of the smoke house. Then for three weeks, a smoke was kept continuously going beneath it. This smoking was done with hickory chips and sometimes with sassafras. This gave it a fine flavor. Sometimes meat was left in salt or put down in ashes through the summer to keep off skippers. There were always plenty of fine hams to be found in the old smoke house, especially throughout the summer. Sausage was also made at butchering time and put up in shucks and hung with the meat (in *A Study of the Home and Local Crafts of the Pioneers of Washington County, Arkansas*, pp. 52–53).

Until very recently hog-killing was a communal activity. Vance Randolph describes a typical gathering during the early years of the twentieth century:

The neighbors all gathered on the appointed day, and unless there was a very large spring nearby they repaired to the nearest creek and built a great fire of logs, in which a number of large stones were heated. Having no vessels big enough to scald hogs in, they diverted the stream into a suitable hollow or pit among the rocks, and heated the water thus impounded by throwing the hot stones into it. When the hogs were scalded everybody helped to scrape and gut the animals, which were then cut up by the most proficient butchers in the party. At noon the women provided a big dinner, with fresh pork of all kinds, and the host set out a jug or two of corn whiskey. In the evening there was another big feed, followed by a dance or a play-party. A certain creek-bottom near Eureka Springs, Arkansas, is still known as "Hawg Scald," because it was a favorite place for these hog-killing festivals (in *The Ozarks: An American Survival of Primitive Society,* pp. 31–32).

Although such "festivals" are rare now, hog-butchering is still an important source of family food supplies.

Beef is more prominent now than it once was, primarily because methods of preservation other than drying have been developed. Fish and wild game, such as turkeys, squirrels, deer, and possum, are also important sources of meat, although few families today use wild game as a major portion of their yearly food supply.

In the nineteenth century, Ozark housewives came up with some interesting ways of creating diversity in the family's diet. One very popular food that is still made by some women was egg butter. This was the result of putting several eggs into a gallon of molasses, which was then stirred until it thickened. Even today many people will attest that egg butter "makes some of the finest eating I have ever had."

Soap Making

Soap making was a skill of special importance in early Ozark homes. The producing of such a necessary item was an economical move, because none of the ingredients involved had to be purchased. Soap making was done in middle-to-late March or early April. By that time many meat scraps, wastes from meat trimmings, and cracklings saved from the rendering of lard at butchering time were available as the fat that was combined with lye to make the yearly soap supply. The first step, taken care of by men during the winter, was carrying the ashes that accumulated in the fireplace and depositing them in the ash hopper. These deposits were kept covered until the housewife was ready to make soap.

Once the cover was thrown back from the hopper, buckets of water were thrown on the ashes until they were completely saturated. The water then began to drip through and escape via a trough at the hopper's base. The resulting liquid, known as lye, was a dark reddish-brown color with a sharp, biting taste. This solution was then saturated with more water until a lighter-colored liquid with a less distinct taste was created. This was called "weak lye." The housewife used one of several methods to determine the strength of the lye. If it would strip a feather, eat up a shuck, or float an ear of corn, it was ready for making soap.

An individual slant on soap making was provided by Mrs. Will Moore of Cane Hill, Arkansas, in 1929. As her commentary makes clear, there were certain beliefs about how and when to make soap, but not everyone subscribed to these ideas:

I used to put a large dishpanful of cracklings and meat scraps into a large twenty-gallon, old fashioned kettle and then pour in the lye until the kettle was nearly filled. Then I would keep that going with a fire underneath it and sometimes have to cook it about all day before it made soap. Later, I learned that heat was necessary only to get the soap grease to a very high temperature; so now, for a great many years, I have always put in my grease and cooked it real fast until it almost burns. Then, I began to pour in the lye and continue to cook, and by the time I have my kettle about full, it is soap. This is much easier than the old method of using cold grease.

The soap is allowed to cool and is removed from the kettle. I have three large "old timey" lin-wood [meaning "linden"] soap troughs that I have always kept mine in. Some women used barrels to keep soap in; others had the troughs made by cutting a hollow-tree trunk. My troughs were dug out of lin-wood tree trunks a great many years ago by Mr. Moore, and they have not been moved from where they are now stacked for thirty years or more, nor have they been entirely empty in all that time. I used to make soap every spring when we were all at home, but at present I only make about every two years, but I can make two kettlefuls in one day easy enough. I still save my soap grease from waste-meat scraps and cracklings from lard.

The fact that soap making must be done at a certain time of the moon's changes and stirred only with a sassafras stick, and only one way, and by only one person, is the superstitious part of it. I never did those things, and I have always had success at soap making (in *A Study of the Home and Local Crafts of the Pioneers of Washington County, Arkansas*, pp. 59–60).

Most housewives of today prefer not to make their own soap. Some women, however, prefer the old-fashioned soap and go through the laborious traditional process because they feel lye soap has better cleansing qualities than commercially manufactured soap. Others who used lye soap as youngsters feel it does too good a job of cleaning, having an almost abrasive quality; obviously, these people prefer to buy their soap.

CHAPTER 3

At Work

The Ozarks is one of those places where, according to popular thought and stereotypical notions, traditional arts and crafts abound. Consequently, people find arts and crafts there in abundance, some indigenous to the Ozarks and some the products of craftspeople with no ties to the region who have merely supplied the tourist traffic with desired items. As Vance Randolph and Gordon McCann put it, the problem is with definition: "Are we talking about crafts that are native to the Ozarks, or are the Ozarks becoming a center for all sorts of craftsmen who have moved here recently, motivated by the 'back to nature' movement or the lucrative tourist trade" (in *Ozark Folklore: An Annotated Bibliography*, vol. II, p. 177).

Despite the stereotypes, most Ozark residents have jobs similar to those found in any region of the country. However, some people do earn their living, or at least a portion of it, from the making of objects. This chapter examines some of the more important arts and crafts that Ozarkers have traditionally practiced as a means of earning or enhancing an income. One of the most important of these is blacksmithing.

BLACKSMITHING

Blacksmithing, of course, did not originate in the Ozarks, or even in the United States, but until recently, it was an essential craft in the region. In an era when most people were farmers, the horse was an essential provider of power. The farmer's machinery was relatively simple, and the blacksmith and his skills were vital to a rural community's existence. He was involved in shoeing horses, repairing a wide range of farm and home equipment, and making a number of items used on the farm and in the

Wally Burleson, black-
smith, Yellville, Arkan-
sas (Photo courtesy *The
Ozarks Mountaineer*)

home. In pioneer times housewives cooked their foods on the hearth or in the fireplace. Homes of those who could afford it had at least two large fireplaces, one at either end of the house. Kettles in which food was cooked were hung on hooks suspended from the jambs of the fireplace. Pot hooks, fire tongs, shovels, and andirons, all made by the blacksmith, were used to handle the heavy cooking utensils. Even the cooking pots themselves were made by the blacksmiths.

At one time all of the implements used in tilling the soil, such as plows and hoes, were made in the local blacksmith's shop. He also produced horse shoes, nails, hinges, latches, and a variety of other necessary items. But the smithy's importance was not just a matter of his producing essential products; his shop was often a focal point of the community. The situation described by A. S. Wood of Marion County, Arkansas, was typical in many villages:

I have heard my father say frequently that on his arrival here, Jake Wolf lived at the mouth of Big North Fork where Sammy South, father of Jerry South, lived after the war. Mr. Wolf owned a blacksmith shop and was Postmaster of the post office there. I think this office was called North Fork. I remember my father said that four families lived in Wiley's Cove in what is now Searcy County. Their names were Sam Leslie, the old man Potter who was a blacksmith, the old man

Griffin and Elijah Milton. On Richland Creek which heads up at the foot of the Boston Mountains where Jack Wasson used to live there were Dave Robertson, Vincen Robertson, Joseph Ray and James Jimmison. All these settlers I have named and all those who lived within thirty-five miles of this office received their mail there and a number of them who lived twenty miles distant patronized Wolf's and Potter's blacksmith shops. Newspapers were rarely seen then and there were but a few letters distributed. The mail was due at the post office once a month (in *Turnbo's Tales of the Ozarks*, p. 113).

Blacksmithing is one of the oldest of crafts still practiced, and throughout much of history the smithy has been a highly valued member of society. In medieval Wales the smith was accorded a place of honor alongside the poet and priest in the prince's court. Although today machinery has largely replaced handwork for such activities as blowing the forge fire, the general principles of the craft have not changed since prehistoric times; modern blacksmiths use the same method of forging that was used thousands of years ago. In essence, forging is a moulding process whereby the smith, using hammer, anvil, and other tools, shapes the hot iron, causing the metal to assume the form he wants.

Five main processes are involved in the blacksmith's work: fullering, jumping, welding, bending, and punching. Fullering, also known as drawing down, refers to reducing the thickness of a piece of metal. These are beaten on the anvil with a hammer, but the fuller, a tool shaped like a chisel but with a rounded nose, has to be used for heavier pieces. After fullering, the metal has a wavy appearance that is smoothed with a hammer. Jumping is a process by which the smith gets more metal at one part of the item than at the other, as in making a head for a rivet. One end of a heated rod is beaten down on the anvil or with a hammer until the desired shape is achieved. Welding involves uniting two pieces of metal by heating them to welding temperature (just below melting point) until the items are molten and fused or soft enough to hammer or press together. Bending is very important to smiths who engage in wrought-iron work. Punching, done either with small hand punches or heavy power drills, is an important part of the blacksmith's work. Because the process strains metal, considerable care is necessary in judging which work is suitable for punching.

Blacksmiths use a wide variety of tools. Hammers of various sizes and shapes are the most often used tools. Many smiths consider a four-pound cross-peen hammer the most practical because it is light enough for the smith to work with all day and at the same time heavy enough to do most jobs. There are both hard-faced and soft-faced hammers, the latter being used when the hard-faced hammer would mar the surface of the item being repaired.

Numerous types of tongs—the straight-lipped ones being the most common—are used to hold the hot metal while it is being worked at the forge or anvil. Although these are available from commercial manufacturers, as are most of the other tools, many blacksmiths prefer to make their own. Indeed some, such as Fred Manes of Richland, Missouri, quoted in Rick Bishop's article "Blacksmithing," take great pride in saying, "I never buy a pair of tongs. I forged out every pair" (in *Bittersweet*, spring 1975, p. 34).

Punches and chisels of various types are also important. Punches usually have long handles to keep the smith's hands clear of the work, as most punching is done while the metal is hot. There are two kinds of chisels, hot and cold, and each has many variations. Cold chisels, used for cutting iron while it is cold, come in various widths with thick points. They are used in conjunction with the ball-peen hammer. Hot chisels are longer and slenderer so that the smith's hands can be kept clear of the hot iron.

Swages are top and bottom tools used for working metal into shape. The top swage has to be struck with the sledge hammer and is rodded; the bottom swage fits into the anvil tool hole. Blacksmiths generally make their own swages, which exist in a variety of designs and shapes and are used for making bolts, tools, rods, and similar items. Swage blocks, heavy square or rectangular cast-iron blocks having different sizes of half-round and V-shaped notches on all sides and differently shaped holes in the face, are used to shape heated metal and are frequently placed on a metal stand so as to be at a proper height for working. Many blacksmiths no longer use swages or swage blocks for the simple reason that there is little or no demand for products made on these tools. One Ozark smithy explains, "That was used when those old steam engines had to have bolts—you couldn't buy them. We could make all the bolts they used. All these little places here had a hammer the same that matched all these and you put whatever you're making down in that and take a sledge hammer and drive it in here for the square shoulders next to the head. You make your bolt the size you want it. It was a wonderful tool in its day and I still use it, but it's kinda going out."

The same fate has befallen the mandrel, a hollow cast-iron cone used for rounding up hoops and rings. In Bishop's article, Fred Manes says, "This is a thing we used to use to bend the wagon tire with, curl it around, weld it up and put it on. That's called a mandrel. See how it tapers? That was made to make a hub band—a band that went around the hub of a wagon. We'd drop them down over that and cure them up" (in *Bittersweet*, spring 1975, pp. 35–36).

One of the most important pieces of equipment in the blacksmith's shop is the anvil, and, like most other items used by the smithy, anvils exist in many different designs. The most common anvil type has a flat face with a punching hole and tool hole for the insertion of a swage or cutting tool at the hanging end. The anvil's face has a hardened steel top, and a portion of the face has a rectangular table that continues in a heavy pointed projection. Both the table and projection are of steel or wrought iron without a hard steel cover. This is to enable the blacksmith when cutting iron with a chisel to avoid damaging the chisel edge.

Another essential piece of blacksmith equipment is the hearth, the place where much of the smith's work is carried out. The hearth is made of stone, brick, or cast iron and has a large rectangular container for the fire. A water trough is situated in front of the fire where pieces of iron are cooled while the iron of the bellows or blower enters the hearth at either the side or back. When hand bellows were used, they were fixed at the side with handle projecting over the front of the hearth. This made it possible for the smith to operate the bellows with his left hand while holding the tongs in the fire with his right hand. Nowadays, most smithy shops, except those in outdoor museums, use electrically driven blowers rather than hand bellows.

Beginning about the time of World War Two, blacksmithing went into a decline for several reasons. One of these was that many people left farming between the two world wars. In 1920 65 percent of Americans lived on farms, a percentage that declined sharply over the next two decades. A second factor was that the character of farming changed greatly during this era. After 1920, although the tractor did not completely replace the horse, it became much more prominent, and mass-produced machinery of some complexity replaced the traditional local ploughs, harrows, and other implements.

In the years between the two world wars many blacksmiths went out of business. Those who remained had to be both ingenious and industrious to meet the challenge of changing circumstances. In Jimmy Harrelston's article "I'm as Regular as a Goose A-Going Barefoot," one blacksmith explains how he was able to stay afloat financially:

Sometimes it was hard going for my customers to pay anything. I had to go to California during the Depression to make some money. The bottom was out of everything and I'd been blacksmithing here. It hit other places before it did here. The first year we begin to feel it here, I wasn't afraid. I wasn't afraid of my customers. I done their work for them and charged it to them. But by the next year, there wasn't a thing. They couldn't pay nothing. I shod their horses all through summer and fall when they wanted to do hauling. I had a big pile of old shoes that I'd took off and I'd tell them, "Now you can't use them barefooted. You gather you up some old shoes and I've got a bunch of them." I fit them and I shod, I bet, a hundred horses for those old poor boys on these ridge farms. Didn't even charge it to them. Didn't make no record of them 'cause they couldn't have paid it to save their lives.

But one winter here during that—it was in '35—farmers had brought me in corn and hogs. I had twenty-five hogs and plenty of corn. One old carpenter was here and he hadn't had a job for a year. He just couldn't get a dime's worth of work to do. One day he came down and told me. He said, "Fred, I'm going up to your house and kill a hog and dress him. We've got to have something to eat." And he did. He'd kill one and give me half of it. And sometimes he'd go up there and kill three or four and we'd just pass it around to people with big families. We killed ever one of them.

Boy, that was tough going. A fella that never went through that, he doesn't know what hard picking is. I've come here to the shop many a week during that Depression and not make two dollars. People didn't have it and they couldn't get it.

So I went to California to get me a job. I left here December 13, 1936, and come back in '38. I got a good job there in the oil fields and paid up what I owed here and bought me twenty-five cows when I got back. When I left here, I think me and my wife and boy left here in an old Model A. The best I remember I had about eighty dollars. We took off. But I went to work just as quick as I got there. I'd work at the oil fields five days a week. Then I'd come to town and the blacksmith there in that town, he had mules and horses scattered over the country that he'd go out and shoe. I went out with him quite a while. Then I went out on my own on Saturday and Sunday. I'd go out to those ranches and shoe their horses and sharpen their plows. I made more on Saturday and Sunday than I did the days I was working in the oil fields. Boy, she was tough going then (in *Bittersweet*, spring 1975, p. 40).

One of the means by which blacksmiths managed to stay in business after World War Two was by becoming farriers exclusively. This craft dates back at least to the time of ancient Rome. Farriers fit horses with shoes for the protection of hooves, especially on hard surfaces. This skill involves more than just manual work; the farrier needs a considerable knowledge of the anatomy of the horse's foot, its diseases, and the methods for curing those diseases. Like blacksmithing, the basic techniques of the farrier's work have changed relatively little since ancient times. Most farriers keep their equipment in a special shoeing box.

The shoeing of horses involves a number of steps: the examination of hooves, removal of the old shoes, the cleaning and smoothing of the hooves, and the putting on of the new shoes. Examination of the hooves begins with the forefeet. Usually the farrier lifts each foot and holds it between his knees. In the case of a very nervous horse, the animal's legs are tied and the shoeing performed while the horse is on its back. Removal of old shoes involves first cutting off the nails with a metal piece called a buffer; then the whole shoe is removed with a pair of pincers. Cleaning and smoothing is done with a knife, raps, and hoof parers, until the hoof is flat enough for the shoe. The shoe is then marked in the center, heated in the fire, and bent to a V-shape. It is reheated and shaped to fit the horse's hoof, a process that requires a special shoe-turning hammer that is double-headed, one end being flat and the other slightly convex. Each side of the handle has protruding small heads used for drawing the clip on the front of a shoe. A number of reheatings, filings, and hammerings take place until the shoe is properly fitted. Getting an exact fit is very important because a shoe that is improperly fitted can lame a horse.

A resurgence of interest in blacksmithing occurred about 1965 for a variety of reasons, one being the rise of craft fairs with their markets for handmade products, both traditional and nontraditional. These shows prompted a number of people to get into blacksmithing and led to the establishment of such large enterprises as Stone County Ironworks in Mountain View, Arkansas. This company, established in the 1980s, is reportedly the largest blacksmith shop in the United States. While it sells products around the world, there are many smaller blacksmith operations of one or two persons that are able to stay in business and provide living wages for its employees. Thus, although the blacksmith is no longer the vital person he once was, his craft is still far from dead.

POTTERY

Since the dawn of civilization, wherever there was suitable clay people have used it to make pots; this craft is one of the oldest practiced by human beings. So too it has existed in the Ozarks for centuries, having been introduced by Indians as early as 1,000 B.C. Early white settlers had a pottery tradition as well, one that apparently was independent of and uninfluenced by Indian pottery, although tracing its history is difficult for a variety of reasons. Early potters saw no need to advertise; sources such as the federal census do not list occupations before 1850; and early pottery was often lost because it was not valued as much as silver, glass, and imported ceramics.

The first non-Indian potter in the Ozarks identifiable by name is William S. Crawley, who came to Washington County, Arkansas, in 1845 from his native White County, Tennessee. There he found clay deposits on the Virgil Guthrie farm that were similar to the pipe clay he and his father had used for making pottery in Tennessee. The following year, at the age of eighteen, he returned to Strickler, a small Washington County community, and established a permanent pottery that he ran until 1875. He was known not only in Washington County but all over northwest

Modern potter working
at his wheel (Photo cour-
tesy Ozark Folk Center)

Arkansas, as his wares were distributed over that entire section of the
state. His most popular products were jars, jugs, crocks, churns, and clay
pipes. According to Zillah Cross Peel's article, "Old Pottery Makers of
Hills Recalled," the clay he used was free of grit "and had enough plastic-
ity to being turned by the potter. The clay turned a red or cream color,
and took a good glaze" (in *Arkansas Gazette*, January 16, 1938).

Crawley's kiln was constructed in the back of his log cabin, and the
furnace used was under the floor of his house. During most of the time his
pottery was in operation, Crawley turned out approximately 750 pieces
of pottery anually. Although he had twenty-one children by two wives,
apparently none of them was interested in continuing his work. So, at the
age of forty-seven Crawley closed his highly successful pottery, even
though he lived to be ninety-three. Despite being well known regionally
as a potter, he was never listed as that in census records, his occupation
always being given as farmer.

The next Ozark potter who can be named is Robert A. Caldwell, who
was active as a potter in Missouri by 1860. The following year, he moved
to Cane Hill, Arkansas, leaving there in 1869 to move to Sebastian
County, Arkansas, where he died in 1888, By 1860 a number of other
potters were active in the Ozark section of Arkansas, including George
Washington Cranston and several members of the Donaldson family in

Franklin County, the Cravens in Independence County, John Pearson in Van Buren County, and Abbott L. Todd in Carroll County. However, at no time were there large colonies of potters; in the entire Ozark region there were probably no more than one hundred people making a substantial portion of their income from pottery. Though there was a need for pots, a large number of potters was not required; even given the difficulty of travel in the region, one potter could service a relatively large area. Population was, in all but a few locations, relatively sparse and would not have been able to support numerous potters.

Pottery-making techniques have changed relatively little over the centuries, with the techniques used by modern studio potters differing little from those employed in prehistoric times. One of the most important tasks of the potter is the selection and preparation of clay. Good pottery clay should be free of soluble impurities such as lime, excess sand, and other mineral fragments. The clay needs to be smooth and of the same consistency throughout; in other words, it requires cleaning and manipulation into the proper, even texture. In Peel's article, one of William Crawley's sons described the process his father used: "We would go to the clay bank for clay in the early spring, but if there happened to be late freeze it would all have to be dumped and a new supply brought in. No pottery could be made from frozen clay. We would put the clay in the pen, dry it out with a big wheel roller, grind it to a dust then sieve it, put it through a dirt mill, then place it in a box (in *Arkansas Gazette*, January 16, 1938).

Once the cleaning process is finished, water is added to create a creamy, smooth consistency called slip. This then passes through a silk gauze screening that squeezes out the water, leaving it stiff enough to be formed into balls and thrown on the wheel. Clay has to be much stiffer for heavy, large pots than for small pots or they might sag from their own weight before they are dry enough for firing. The thrower sits on a seat fixed to the framework of the wheel. At the top is a tray containing the prepared balls of clay. The potter first presses to get rid of air holes, then throws the clay ball onto the revolving wheel. Frequently wetting his or her hands, the potter shapes the spinning clay into a tall cone raised and shaped by the fingers and thumb. Slowly the shape is thinned, with the height being checked by means of a homemade gauge; the pot is then removed from the wheel with the help of a wire cutter. It is taken to the drying racks where the pots are dried under artificial heat in the open air. Pots must be thoroughly dried before the firing, because if they contain any moisture they could explode under the extreme heat of the kiln. Before pots are set out to dry they are trimmed with a scraper and all marks removed with a wet sponge.

Pottery has to be carefully stacked in the kiln because no two pots must touch. The pottery needs firing once or twice, depending on the nature of the clay and how the products will be used. Unglazed ware and stoneware are fired only once, while most glazed ware has to be fired twice. After the first firing, the glaze is applied and is fused with the body of the pot during the second firing. Removable bricks are built into the kiln wall so that the potter can see what is happening while the pots are being fired. When the glaze begins fusing, the heat must be reduced.

Three kinds of glaze were known in the nineteenth century. Salt glaze, made with common table salt, was probably the most often used. Slip glazes were also popular, while the ash, or alkaline, glaze was the least common in the Ozarks. Both slip and ash glazes were applied to the "green" pots before firing, while salt glaze occurred during firing. Now salt glazes are considered antiquated by most potters, although art potters still make great use of them. Alkaline glazes, on the other hand, are much more popular now than ever before.

Although there is little definite documentation to support such a claim, it is likely that the most common type of kiln in the nineteenth century was the "groundhog" kiln. A very modest looking structure, it was low and elongated and built into the side of a hill that served as insulation. Another style of kiln that enjoyed some popularity was the "beehive." An updraft kiln, the beehive allowed heat to rise through the chamber and the stacked pottery and out the roof. Both the groundhog and beehive kilns have now been generally replaced by the gas-fired kiln, although some potters use combined forms such as gas-fired beehive kiln.

Traditional potters produced functional, utilitarian items such as churns, jugs, crocks, and jars. They were more concerned with the usefulness of their pottery than with its esthetics. But, by 1900, the small number of local potters had diminished as mass-produced and -distributed wares took sizeable portions of the market, leaving the local potter with a smaller variety of saleable items. Nevertheless, the rural pottery tradition continues to the present, although now it is primarily college- and studio-trained potters who hold to the rural Ozark pottery-making traditions of the past.

GUNSMITHS

In the eighteenth and nineteenth centuries, the gunsmith was a vital craftsman in rural communities, not only in the Ozarks but around the world. He was important because his product was relied on by most families to provide at least a portion of the family's yearly meat supply. During the history of white settlement of the Ozarks, several types of guns were made. The earliest of these was the flintlock musket, which was loaded through the musket of the barrel and used a flint ignition system. The flint, attached to the spring-driven hammer, struck the steel frizzen, sending sparks into a flashpan filled with powder. This powder ignited the main charge, which sent the ball out of the barrel towards the target. By the time of the Civil War, breech-loaded rifles were available but not widely used or made in the Ozarks. A version of the Pennsylvania or Kentucky rifle, which had a longer barrel, smaller bore, and lighter stock, was of more significance in the nineteenth-century Ozarks.

In contrast to those involved in other types of crafts, gunsmiths were plentiful in the Ozarks from an early date. By the 1850s, literally dozens of gunsmiths were active, and probably others worked at the trade part time but considered their main occupation something else. For example, Independence County, Arkansas, had seven gunsmiths by 1870. Even a sparsely populated county like Searcy in Arkansas had one full-time gunsmith by the time of the Civil War, while by 1870 Washington County, Arkansas, one of the most populous in the Ozark region of the state, had ten. Of course, the Civil War heightened the need for weapons and obviously led to a rise in the number of gunsmiths. Some of these craftsmen, such as John Pearson, became quite famous. A native of England, Pearson learned his craft in Baltimore before moving to western Arkansas. His fame comes primarily from his association with inventor Samuel Colt, who according to R. L. Wilson's book *The Colt Heritage*, referred to Pearson as his "number one gunsmith and consultant in developing the first revolvers" (quoted in *Arkansas Made*, vol. I, p. 170). Unfortunately, relations between the two men soured and their association was terminated.

Like many other craftsmen, the old-time gunsmiths have lost much of their market to mass production. Even so, there are still customers who prefer locally produced guns, which means that gunsmiths are not likely to disappear anytime in the foreseeable future. One aspect of their approach that has changed, however, is the greater importance of esthetics today. While old-time gunsmiths liked to produce a good-looking gun, the matter of how pleasing it was to the eye was less important than how well it functioned as a gun. Modern gunsmiths, even those who are very traditional in most respects, consider the instrument's beauty to be as important as its performance.

BASKET MAKING

As far as can be determined, the Indian tribes in the Ozarks had no basket-making tradition; if they did, it has had no influence on current Ozark basketry. That basket-making tradition is derived exclusively from Appalachian basketry, which dates it to the 1840s. Although some crafts-

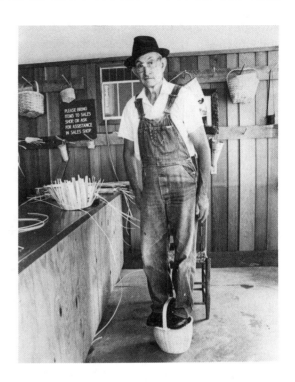

Wayman Evans (1913–1993), renowned basket maker from Floral, Arkansas (Photo courtesy Ozark Folk Center)

men in the past depended on their baskets for a livelihood, there were never great numbers of basket makers. At the present time several persons earn their living producing baskets, most of them being members of basket-making families. The most famous of these are the Gibsons of northwestern Arkansas who, according to family tradition, started making baskets several generations ago when a blind basket weaver taught one of their ancestors.

Basket making requires a relatively small amount of equipment: a cutting tool, and a pair of hands. Every craftsman, however, has personal preferences in tools, some of which are homemade and traditional. Most basketmakers use a maul and wedges, a froe, a shaving horse, and drawknife. The maul and wedges are used in splitting a log into quarters or eighths, after which the outer bark is removed. A froe is used to split each piece into fourths, and the shaving horse holds the piece while a drawknife is used to trim it to a smooth board as thick as the splints are to be wide. A knife is then used to separate the splints. Once the appropriate number of splints are available, weaving begins and the result is a complete basket.

Although at one time hickory, ash, and white oak were all used in producing baskets, now white oak is preferred. Some basket makers, however, use imported flat reed because it is inexpensive and saves a lot of work. Among the numerous types of baskets commonly made in the Ozarks are gizzard baskets, egg baskets, flower baskets, clothes baskets, and half-bushel baskets. Heart-shaped handles are a common feature of Ozark baskets. Interestingly, rib-type baskets are much less common in the Ozarks than in Appalachia, even though that is where the basket-making tradition comes from.

At one time basket makers hawked their wares by traveling on horse-back around a relatively small region. Now most basket makers either have their own sales shops, ship through the mail, or distribute their wares through amusement parks, such as Silver Dollar City, or craft organizations, such as the Arkansas Craft Guild, or regionwide organizations, such as the Ozark Folk Center. However the products are sold, what is important is that the tradition of basket making remains alive and vital.

WOOD CARVING

One Ozark craft that has received a great deal of attention in recent years is wood carving. In his article for the book *The Craftsman in America*, the late Clay Anderson, longtime editor of *The Ozarks Mountaineer*, empha-sized wood carving above all other traditional Ozark crafts. Yet, the skill of wood carving seems to be mainly of recent vintage in the Ozarks, mostly dating from the 1960s. Carver Eppes Mabry told researcher Don-ald Van Horn in 1977: "I can't remember of anybody just actually carv-ing, only sitting around up town, the old-timers sit round and whittle on a stick of cedar. They'd be some of them with a walking cane. They have a piece of cedar maybe three foot long, they'd put a ball in the end of it. Some of the older people would. I used to whittle out walking stick with a snake, you know, going around the stick. Be sitting around and git tired waiting on a deer come along. I git me a something and start whittling on it" (in *Carved in Wood: Folk Sculpture in the Arkansas Ozarks*).

Though it is meager, there is evidence of some wood carving activity before the 1960s. In 1958 Ernie Deane, an *Arkansas Gazette* columnist, wrote an article about V. L. Hill of Rogers, Arkansas, who made wood carvings of animals that he sold to gift shops. However, a major increase in wood carving in the Ozarks occurred after 1960. Various government programs and the rise of a crafts movement, both of which were designed to improve economic conditions in the area, were the catalysts of this change. Leo Rainey, one of the original organizers of the Ozark craft movement, provides a brief history:

Back in 1959 this area was a pilot area in rural development work. Now this came back in earlier years during the Eisenhower administration; they implemented a

Jim Nelson, Three
Brothers, Arkansas,
carving a spirit face
(Photo courtesy Ozark Folk
Center)

rural development program. First Arkansas in '55 started five pilot counties. The extension service put out a person in each of five counties. Now then, they decided nationally that you could do more on a regional basis, so in '59 this was one of the few areas in the United States that had an area agent, a regional and several counties agents. They met a lot, and they did labor surveys and a lot of preliminary things trying to get jobs and tourism was recognized as one of the big opportunities (in *Carved in Wood*, p. 28).

It is hardly surprising that those interested in bringing economic benefits to the Ozarks through crafts looked towards southern Appalachia. Several decades earlier, traditional arts and crafts had been seen as a way of helping Appalachian mountaineers financially. A contingent of people from the Ozarks visited Gatlinburg, Tennessee, to study the activities of the Southern Highland Handicraft Guild and concluded that a similar system would work in the Ozarks. Thus, the Ozark Foothills Handicraft Guild was established in the early 1960s, one of its missions being to promote wood carving and other crafts with workshops. While not all wood carvers have developed as a direct result of the Guild's activities, it has been the single greatest influence.

Most observers agree that the Ozark Foothills Handicraft Guild (since renamed Arkansas Craft Guild) has been successful in its original goal of upgrading the economic standards of the region. This success, however, is seen by many as a mixed blessing. Donald Van Horn, whose book is one of the best on Ozark traditional wood carving, says that economic success has resulted in the debasement of "the art of woodcarving as a traditional form of expression of folk culture. In many instances, the integrity of the art has been sacrificed for commercial gain" (in *Carved in Wood*, p. 31).

Amusement parks such as Silver Dollar City, Missouri, and other shops catering primarily to the tourist trade help sustain a number of Ozark wood carvers. These places sell various types of carvings, many of them nontraditional, ranging from tiny wooden shoes to almost life-size cigar-store Indians (usually dressed as plains Indians not as Ozarks Indians), to "hillbilly" caricatures. As one of the most influential persons involved in promoting this form of wood carving says, "We are a business here. We are creating a market for these people to sell their work" (in *Carved in Wood*, p. 34).

A relatively small number of tools are used by wood carvers, usually including a knife, gouge, and scraper. The other necessity is wood, and each carver has his own preferences about which woods are best for specific carvings. Junior Cobb of Three Brothers, Arkansas, likes sassafras, walnut, and even driftwood. Some carvers work almost exclusively with basswood, while others prefer different species. Birds are one of the most popular forms turned out by Ozark wood carvers. Animals, Ozark people, and "spirit faces," which, according to some wood carvers, is a motif borrowed from Indian tradition, are other favorite subjects.

BROOM MAKING

Broom making is another traditional craft that was revived by the 1960s crafts movement. At one time almost every farm grew broomcorn and, often, members of farm families made their own brooms. These were generally very crude, consisting of several bunches of broomcorn heads that

Woodcarving school at Compton Ridge, Missouri, 1991 (Photo courtesy *The Ozarks Mountaineer*)

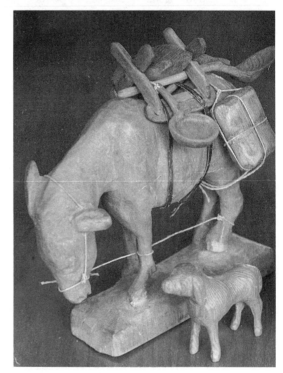

Mule and dog, woodcarving (Photo courtesy *The Ozarks Mountaineer*)

had been stripped of seeds. These brooms were generally round, rather than flat, with the flat brooms developing around 1820. Most often these brooms were made by women; such broom makers were called jack-leg broom makers, meaning that they didn't do it for a living. Now broom makers are generally men, and broomcorn is rarely available from local farms. For a period of time most Ozark broom makers purchased their broomcorn from Illinois, but now it usually comes from Mexico because prices there are lower than elsewhere.

The broom maker's tools are few; they consist of a workbench, called a broom horse, a pair of pliers, scissors, a bladed draw knife, hammer, wire cutters, and broom needles. Not all of these tools are needed for every broom, and broom makers who specialize in only one or two types of brooms may never use some of these tools. The techniques for making each type of broom differ slightly. Of the brooms commonly made by Ozark broom makers, the most popular is probably the turkey wing, or the fantail, as it is known in some regions. In earlier times real turkey wings were sometimes used as brooms, but they have long been supplanted by brooms that somewhat resemble the shape of turkey wings.

When making any type of broom it is necessary to soften the broomcorn by soaking it in hot water. The corn must then be used immediately or it will mold, mildew, and ruin. The corn is sorted before the actual broom construction begins. When the turkey wing is being made, bunches of corn are placed on a table in the form of a cross, with other bunches criss-crossed on the right-hand cross. Then the weaving of wire begins, with several turns made until the long loose end of the wire is buried in the center of the corn. To this core other bunches of corn are added and the process of tightening the wire is repeated each time. Once this process is completed, the handle is plaited and the broom is trimmed, both by scissors and knife, and the turkey wing broom is ready.

Most broom makers active in the Ozarks today were influenced either directly or indirectly by William Henry Young, a native of eastern Kentucky. Young learned traditional broom making from his mother and acquired additional knowledge at Berea College in Berea, Kentucky, under the guidance of Robert E. Lee Bottom, who learned broom making living in the Shaker community at Pleasant Hill, Kentucky. In 1971 Young, acting on the suggestion of Leo Rainey, taught a workshop in broom making in Mountain View, Arkansas. In his book *Buy a Broom Besom: The Story of a Broom*, Young briefly describes his experience:

It was at the Arkansas Folk Festival of 1971, Leo convinced me I could teach a course in broom making. . . . That was in April; I arrived in June to teach the course. By this time, I was convinced I could not do the job.

I faced ten men and one young lady, Susie Roll; the preparations had been made; the students were there; I had a contract to teach; I was on the scene; and so was Leo, with a cocked gun. I had nowhere to run. Teach I must. For five, long, hot days we made brooms, tore them apart, made and re-made. I know at times each of those who stayed with me for the entire week must have blessed me out in their minds numerous times. The instructions were complete with nothing left to chance; the only thing was practice, practice, practice. The men at first thought Susie would leave after the first day. We did have drop outs, but not Susie. She learned all of the five types of brooms I taught, and the men voted her fantail broom the best one of the class. I never felt I would make the week, but Jimmy and Billy Ford, D. L. Humphres, Harold Hansford, and Mr. and Mrs. Clarence Young (no relation), along with Leo's cocked gun, kept me to my task. Leo told me as I was leaving Arkansas, I was leaving behind a re-kindled craft and the Guild has some good broom makers (p. 30).

Bill Ford is still an active broom maker, as was his father, Jimmy, until his death in 1993. Most of those Ozark craftsmen who started making brooms recently learned from the Fords or from some other members of Young's 1971 workshop.

COOPERING

Not much can be said about the craft of coopering as practiced in the Ozarks since virtually no research has been done on the subject. To date only one article on the subject has appeared; it was one page long and was published sixty-six years ago. In that brief paper, "Uncle Matt, the Cooper," poet Mary Elizabeth Mahnkey discussed the work of a cooper near Kirbyville, Missouri, who made barrels, buckets, piggins, and churns. Mahnkey described him as a very skilled craftsman, noting that a "cedar churn made by him was so perfectly joined, so smoothly finished with sandpaper, that it might well pass for a piece of pottery" (in *Missouri Magazine*, November, 1929, p. 29).

The lack of public attention does not mean that coopering has been unimportant historically. Even though the story of its existence in the Ozarks has yet to be detailed, it is safe to assume that the craft had a period of prominence, particularly in places like Leslie, Arkansas, where there were at one time several stave mills. Coopering is one of the oldest of crafts, being mentioned several times in the Bible and practiced in ancient Egypt and Rome. Roman invaders brought the craft to the British Isles where it still flourishes, albeit on a small scale. In this work, unlike in many other crafts, machine techniques have not replaced the traditional methods.

Considering its long history and the need for many of the products, it is reasonable to assume that coopering once flourished on a broad scale in the Ozarks. At the same time, it seems unlikely that the number of coopers active in the region was ever extremely large, both for economic reasons and because of the complexity of the craft. There are three categories of coopering—dry coopering, white coopering, and wet coopering—and it is probable that all three were practiced in the Ozarks. Dry coopering consists of building casks to hold nonliquid substances, such as flour, fruit, and vegetables. Since it is known that housewives solved the problem of storing foodstuffs in part by barrel storage, it is reasonable to assume that dry coopering was practiced in the region. Moreover, the sole published reference to Ozark coopering says that barrels of this type were part of the craftsman's output. White coopering, the making of pails, butter churns, washtubs, and other utensils for dairy and household use, is thought to have disappeared completely by the 1930s. Mahnkey's article verifies that this form of coopering was still practiced in the Ozarks in the early twentieth century. Wet coopering is concerned with the manufacturing of casks that can hold liquid substances.

The favorite types of wood used in coopering are oak, sycamore, ash, elm, poplar, and beech. Wet coopers use oak exclusively, while sycamore and ash in addition to oak are preferred by white coopers. The dry cooper uses a greater variety of woods than other coopers. The cooper's tools are numerous but can be categorized as falling into seven types: shaping tools; trussing tools, used to hold staves in shape once they have been bent to the barrel's shape; topping tools, used to shape the ends of the cask to provide places for the barrel's cover pieces to fit; cleaning tools, which clean and smooth the inside and outside of the cask; bunging tools, for boring the bung hole and smoothing away its jagged edges; heading tools, for shaping a barrel's head; and hooping tools, which are used to cut, put in place, and shape the barrel's iron hoops.

The fact that coopering is an arduous, complicated task may have led to its decline in the Ozarks. While there are a few coopers active in the region today, primarily practicing dry and white coopering, they do not represent an unbroken tradition but are revivalists who, in almost every instance, work for amusement parks or museums.

DOLL MAKING

One folk art originally practiced without thought of financial profit was doll making. At the present time, various types of dolls are made, but only two—cornshuck dolls and applehead dolls—have proven to be very profitable with the tourist trade in the Ozarks. It has long been assumed that white settlers learned the skill of making cornshuck dolls from

American Indians, particularly tribes in the Northeast, with the knowledge spreading to other parts of the United States. This theory seems to be mainly based on the fact that Indians introduced corn to the world.

Materials used in making cornshuck dolls are relatively few and easily obtained. Dry corn shucks, of course, are the most important, with other essential items being a bowl of warm water (for keeping the shucks damp so they will not break while the doll is being constructed), scissors, string, pipecleaner or wire, straight pins, and glue. The ready availability of the materials and the relative ease with which these dolls can be made partly explains why this form of doll making has become popular, but the most important reason is the considerable public demand.

Except for conventional dolls (such as stuffed dolls) only one of the doll forms made by Ozark artisans, the applehead doll, has gained widespread acceptance. When the apples are dried, they take on various shapes depending on the action of lemon juice and alum on the fruit. Thus, it is impossible to make two identical applehead dolls. Very little equipment is required; in addition to the apples, lemon juice, and alum, a knife is essential.

MUSICAL INSTRUMENTS

For at least a century and a half many kinds of musical instruments have been produced by Ozark craftsmen. These include fiddles, banjos, guitars, hammered dulcimers, mountain dulcimers, and others. It is technically inaccurate to call most of these instrument builders craftsmen, because their skills are learned in very formal ways and their techniques are standardized. The makers of the mountain dulcimer, however, are an exception; this instrument is a folk instrument in the strictest sense. Until recently there were no mountain dulcimer "factories" turning the instrument out on a mass scale. A few such companies now exist, but even these don't turn dulcimers out in volume like auto assembly lines. Before the 1960s there were few persons attempting to market mountain dulcimers, with most builders making only a few for themselves or their families. A person who made as many as six instruments in a lifetime was considered a prolific dulcimer maker. Finally, there were, and are, no standards used in the construction of mountain dulcimers—no standard measurements, no specific woods that must be used, no rules regarding any other aspect of construction. Builders traditionally used whatever materials were at hand, ranging from baling wire for fretboards to turkey or goose quills for the plectrum. (Further information about the dulcimer is given in the section on musical instruments in chapter 5.)

THE OZARK JOHNBOAT

Probably the most famous craft product created in the Ozarks is the wooden johnboat. Although these are now largely displaced by aluminum johnboats, there are still a few people who prefer the original wooden variety. Who actually created the first johnboat is unknown, but tradition says that it was originally designed by a man named John to be used for float trips on the White River. As nice a story as that makes, it probably isn't accurate. Some people think Charlie and John Barnes, two brothers who are considered among the greatest Ozark river guides, created the first johnboat. If so, the johnboat can not be much more than a century old. However, it is probably impossible to determine for certain who the inventor was. What is known is that generations of people have used the boat.

The johnboat is a long, narrow, flat-bottomed boat designed for fishing the pools of Ozark rivers and for floating over the swift, shallow streams. While the boats were used throughout the region, individual variations were numerous because the boats were adapted to the special characteristics of each river. In Ellen Gray Massey's book, *Bittersweet Country*, Emmitt Massey, a long-time johnboat builder, discusses the characteristics of the boat:

They were a heavy, durable boat made strictly for floating and fishing Ozark rivers. They were long, I've heard of some as long as twenty-seven feet to haul freight on Current River, but most around here were sixteen to twenty feet. The longer they are the most buoyancy they have. I wouldn't want one less than sixteen feet. They were designed to be stable enough to stand upright in while fishing and to float in four inches of water. They are narrow to go through brush and around log jams. Each boat I make, I do it a little different. Many people will disagree with me on building this boat, but this is my way now. Another time maybe I'd make it completely different (p. 287).

Wooden johnboats are considerably heavier than aluminum ones, but this is advantageous in two ways. One is that they make less noise in the water and the other is that the heavier boat is easier to maneuver. Mahogany, linden, butternut, black gum, and redwood are the woods most often used in making johnboats. In the days before power tools were generally available, builders made the boats' floors by simply butting the edges together. If the boats were kept in the water, they were relatively leakproof. Most johnboat builders kept their boats in the river until they wore out because that caused the wood to stay wet and free of leaks. Once a boat started leaking constantly, it would be converted into a feed trough, or given some other use, and a new johnboat would be built. The fact that aluminum boats are less prone to leak is undoubtedly one of the major reasons why they have generally replaced the wooden johnboats.

PEARLING

Pearling was a skill that provided a significant source of income for many families living along the Black and White rivers in northern Arkansas. Dr. J. H. Myers of Black Rock, Arkansas, founded the pearling industry in 1897 when he found a valuable pearl two miles upstream from Black Rock. Soon Black Rock on the Black River and Newport on the White River became the greatest pearl markets in the nation. Between 1897 and 1902 a total of $1,271,000 was paid out to people along the two rivers for pearls and shells. A button factory was also established at Black Rock that remained active until the 1940s. At that time the availability of cheaper plastic buttons from Japan wiped out the industry.

In 1936 Walter McLeod described how pearls were harvested:

At first when a supply of mussels could be found in the shallow waters over the bars, the method of getting them out was to wade in and get them with the bare hands or with forks. Some persons who did not like to go into the water would sit on the banks and hire some one to go in and bring the mussels out to them, or they might buy them at so much per hundred. Later when the supply of mussels in shallow water became scarce boats and tongs, made of two cotton seed forks with tines cut off to half the regular length, were used. There was then a great falling off in the number of pearl hunters.

During the first year or so, no effort was made to save the mussel shells. They were dumped into the river or left on the banks. Later it was found that the shells could be sold at $7 to $10 per ton, and digging shells was taken up as an occupation by many men. If they found a pearl, they were that much ahead (in *Centennial Memorial History of Lawrence County*, p. 82).

Although the major pearling activity ended fifty years ago, a few men still gather shells. In 1979 Bert and Mildred Hicks interviewed one of these pearlers, Willis McMullen, and described his technique in their article "Pearling on the Black River":

He showed us the "crow's feet" used for gathering shells, and a handful of slugs left over from previous shelling trips. The crow's feet apparatus is a 10-foot bar with hooks hanging from it like a trotline. The bar is fastened to the side of the boat which drifts downstream. Mussels open to latch onto the hooks and are drawn up into the boat. . . . When we got there, McMullen had a fire going under a washtub . . . Some of the mussels were in the steaming water to make them open easily; others had been in the water and were ready to open, and others were still to be steamed.

McMullen said some people eat the clam-like meat inside, but it is tough and tasteless. He and his friends were going to use this lot for catfish bait.

We watched with interest as they opened the shells, admiring each little slug that was found, and the exquisite rainbow colors lining the insides of the shells. When the beautiful little pearl emerged, we were as proud and delighted as parents (in *The Ozarks Mountaineer*, December 1980, p. 66).

At one time the crafts discussed in this chapter represented a major source of income for many Ozark residents. While there are still a number of people who practice these skills, in most cases the work is considerably less important economically than it once was. For example, a century ago, every town, even those of fewer than five hundred people, would have at least one blacksmith shop. Now, with the exception of a town like Mountain View, Arkansas, with its Stone County Ironworks and the Ozark Folk Center, one has to search to find blacksmiths in most Ozark towns. Another change during the past century is that a greater number of people are engaged in these crafts on a part-time basis. Although some skills, such as pearling, were apparently never considered by most practitioners as anything other than a spare-time source of supplemental income, that was not the case with blacksmithing, broom making, coopering, and similar crafts. There is now an increasing number of craftsmen who produce a variety of craft products on a spare-time basis.

It would be erroneous to think that the "work" crafts are dying; at least one of the crafts discussed here—wood carving—is currently enjoying its highest level of historic and economic importance. As noted earlier, this is largely the result of the recent and heavily promoted crafts revival movement in the Ozarks. Although this movement rekindled interest in other crafts, its greatest beneficiary seems to be wood carving.

CHAPTER 4

Folk Customs

While some Ozark customs deal with work, recreation, and social events, most either pertain to the life cycle and rites of passage, such as birth, marriage, and death, or are calendar customs, which means they are associated with holidays. Actually, many customs concerning the life cycle involve belief in magic or the supernatural and thus technically are not customs but beliefs or superstitions. An example is the idea, once common among the hillfolk, that an ax placed under the bed of a woman in labor will make the birth easier. Another is the practice of peeling an apple in one piece and throwing the peel on the floor where it supposedly would form the first initial of a girl's future husband. An even more elaborate example is the dumb supper. The following story, told by Mary Elizabeth Mahnkey, was originally printed in the *White River Leader* in Branson, Missouri, in 1934. Mahnkey said the story was told and believed in Taney County, Missouri, when she was a girl.

A dear friend of mother's a plump and jolly woman, comforting and reposeful, not one capable of harboring such strange and weird beliefs, told the story of the dumb supper, so vividly, so impressively, that I never forgot. She and mother were quilting and as the story progressed, and she would bend her face to bite off her thread, she got in the way of giving a cautious glance over her shoulder, and before the tale had ended, I, too, was giving rather awed glances out into the long, darksome hall.

She was talking as if she had been present, or as if she had intimately known the parties engaged in this supernatural feast. It seemed the family were away for the night, and the grown girls, left in charge of the home, had invited in some neighbor girls to keep them company, so a dumb supper was proposed. This meant, that in utter silence, and every step taken, to be made backwards, the table was to be laid for a guest, who would come in at midnight, and who was to be the future husband of the girl at whose plate he sat down. The table was only set for one, as it seemed at the test, only one girl was grave enough to thus put her fortune to the trial.

The others watched her in fascinated silence, as she stepped quickly, if awkwardly, about her task, in the big low ceilinged kitchen. She placed a peculiar knife at the side of the mysterious guest's plate, with a roguish smile at her friends. A sharpbladed knife, set into a piece of deer horn, for one handle.

In utter silence they waited, until the old clock slowly droned out the 12 strokes of midnight, when to their terror, the door was dashed open, a tall form advanced, with swift noiseless steps, and then—an icy wind blew out the light, and one of the horrified girls screamed. But one braver than the rest, closed the door and lighted the lamp. No spectral visitor, they were alone, but the maiden who had set the table, pointed with white face and shaking hands, the peculiar old knife was not there.

Later, this girl did marry a stranger, who had come, as a visiting cousin, to the home of a nearby neighbor. And they seemed to be very happy, although the man was very quiet, even taciturn.

One day the girl's mother, going across the ridge to visit her, found the little cabin strangely cold and forbidding, and hurried in, to find her daughter lying as if dead, with a knife thrust into her breast.

When at last help had been summoned, and the old backwoods doctor, able surgeon was he, too, brought her back to consciousness, shudderingly she told the story.

In a moment of girlish confidence she had told the story of the dumb supper, and the strange guest, "as tall as you," she had said, and he had listened, in sinister silence. Then he went to an old leather valise he always kept locked, unlocked it, took something in his hand and said to her coldly, "And you are the one. You are that witch. That night I walked through hell," and thrust the knife into her breast, and ran from the house. He was never seen again, and the knife was the same old peculiar knife with the deer horn handle and the keen blade, that the thoughtless girl had laid when so careless and gay, she had set the dumb supper (in *Ozark Magic and Folklore*, pp. 180–81).

There are, however, true folk customs associated with courtship, marriage, birth, and death, although none are as unusual as the dumb supper and none are unique to the Ozarks.

CUSTOMS PERTAINING TO BIRTH

Probably the most common customs concerning birth are the dressing of male babies in blue and female babies in pink and the passing out of cigars by the father after the baby's arrival. At one time many people wrapped a newborn baby boy in his father's shirt and a baby girl in her mother's petticoat. These practices, which were to bring the child good luck, have virtually disappeared. Some customs concerning birth are not taken too seriously even by those who practice them. An example is the custom of offering a baby boy a bottle, a coin, and a Bible. It is said that if he grabs the bottle first, he will be a drunkard; if the coin, he will be involved in some business pursuit; if the Bible, he will be either a preacher or a very religious man. This is now basically a joking custom, when it is practiced at all, and possibly always was.

COURTSHIP AND MARRIAGE CUSTOMS

Many customs concerning courtship and marriage that involved divination were never widely popular and have now generally been abandoned. This is the case with one method girls used to find out who their future mate would be: "They tell me that sometimes a girl writes the names of six boys on six slips of paper and puts them under her pillow. When she awakes in the night, she pulls out one at random and throws it on the floor. She does not look at it until daylight, when it will be found to bear the name of her future husband" (in *Ozark Magic and Folklore*, p. 175).

Some Ozark courtship customs were also calendar customs because they were practiced only on a specific holiday. Such was the nineteenth-century custom of boys leaving small boxes of fruit and candies at their sweethearts' doorsteps on the eve of Valentine's Day. If they were very brave, the young men left a pickle with the sweets. An element of magic was involved because, according to tradition, any girl who ate a Valentine pickle was thereafter unable to resist the boy who had given it to her.

Other Ozark courting customs are less exotic. Until recently, the idea of "going Dutch" was unpopular in the Ozarks. Males were looked upon as the ones who should provide whatever money was needed, and any boy expecting the girl to shoulder part of the expenses was viewed negatively by most of his friends. Actually, expenses were not a great consideration until recently, because most dating took place in the girl's home, or at church, dances, play-parties, or similar venues, most of which cost little or nothing. Once a couple started going together, they were expected to forego any other romantic attachments; to do otherwise was considered bad form. Of course, a girl's receiving of an engagement ring was a formal notice of the couple's status.

After the engagement is announced, the prospective bride is given a shower, perhaps several, in which she receives gifts from friends. Occasionally, stag parties are held for the groom, but this is a relatively recent phenomenon in the Ozarks. Even now, they are not as common as bridal showers. Other celebrations involving the bride and groom are reserved for after the wedding. At one time the infare was popular and was often elaborate. Basically a housewarming, it was usually held in the newlywed couple's home, although it sometimes took place elsewhere. James Masterson discusses an infare held in Arkansas in the 1840s that was described in the popular magazine *Spirit of the Times*:

The host, as he tells us, "fixed up my old musket and started out to kill some provisions for the infair," and his efforts were rewarded with a fat deer and two fine turkeys. He provided, also, a jug of new rye whisky. In the meantime, "The old woman and the gals went around to the neighbor's houses to borrow things, and get them to come over and help." The result of preparations so thorough was a supper which "had the character of taking the rag off the bush over anything that had ever taken place in them parts for nine years." After the repast all the young men kissed the bride, and the dancing began. The host was unable to provide the music himself; the strings of his fiddle had been devoured by ticks, and his bow had been scorched when he used it to stir some coffee-berries which were being roasted in the ashes. But Cousin John Overton had brought along his new fiddle, and he played the *Highland Fling* with such energy that every clap-board began to rattle. The frolic continued almost until dawn (in *Arkansas Folk-lore*, p. 134).

Infares remained popular in the Ozarks until well into the twentieth century but have now disappeared, their place being taken by less elaborate events such as shivarees. Shivarees usually do not occur until some time after the wedding. At one time lasting for hours and occasionally getting rough, nowadays they last only for two to three hours, and the pranks are mild. A shivaree held in Stone County, Arkansas, in 1983 consisted of friends descending on the couple's house at nine o'clock in the evening and staying for about two hours. The evening's entertainment consisted of the groom being carried around the house on a rail, fire-crackers being set off, a great deal of hollering by the men in attendance, and singing by the various guests.

According to an anonymous contributor to the *Spirit of the Times*, writing in the 1840s, and to Marion Hughes, writing in the first decade of the twentieth century, some weddings were less-than-elaborate affairs. However, it should be kept in mind that both writers were striving for humor (in Hughes's case many readers saw nothing funny in his comments). The 1840s writer describes the scene after the couple have been pronounced husband and wife:

A puncheon table, with two sheets for a cloth—was spread in the other room, and the happy crowd proceeded to luxuriate themselves. On the table were four large cakes equidistant from each other—handsomely iced, with holes in the centre, in which were inserted four large yellow tallow candles. After partaking of the chickens, bacon, venison &c, I proceeded to aid our hostess in "handing the cake." While she took the ginger cake and dough nuts, I, with the knife in hand, attacked one of the four large cakes; I had hardly finished the cutting part when our hostess took me by the arm and whispered in my ear, "that's not to eat." Having "watered my mouth" for a piece, I was determined to have it anyhow, and forthwith took a large mouthful; but I was like the boy who in attempting to steal a drink of molasses swallowed a cup of soft soap; I had got my mouth full of *white washed corn bread* instead of iced wedding cake (in *Arkansas Folklore*, p. 133).

Even more humble was the Polk County, Arkansas, wedding discussed by Hughes:

The neighbors gathered in, and the women was all in the house, the girl had washed with boughten soap, and put on her new dress, and combed her hair, and they were all sitting around and picking wool, and the men were all out in the edge of the woods, and had a logheap built up, and was all standing around telling yarns.

When the preacher and the young man to be slaughtered arrived on the scene, they went right in, of course. The men all followed them, and the little log house was jam full of sight seers.

When they went in, the young lady, the bride, had a big hunk of wool, picking away as unconcerned as any of them. The preacher made them stand up right in front of the fireplace, with their backs to the fire, and face the crowd, while he proceeded with the ceremony.

But the bride did not lay down her wool; she kept on picking while he was swearing in the young man. But when he asked her if she would care for him in sickness and cook for him in health, and be his wife the remainder of her life, she stopped picking wool, studied for a minute, took a snuff stick out of her mouth, turned around, spit a stream of tobacco juice into the fire, and said, "I reckon." Then he pronounced them man and wife.

Inside of fifteen minutes they had kicked the dogs out doors, rolled the pumpkins under the bed, set the chairs around the wall, tuned up the fiddle, mated out two sets, and was dancing.

You could have heard them a mile. They didn't stop for supper. When one would get hungry they would run out in the shed kitchen and eat a roasted sweet potato, wash it down with a cup of branch water, take a fresh chaw of tobacco and go on with the dance (in *Three Years in Arkansaw*, pp. 70–71).

It is safe to assume that most Ozarkers of the early twentieth century did not have as nonchalant an attitude towards their wedding as the bride described by Hughes. Today, most weddings are followed by some sort of celebration, although not by infares, shivarees, or any similar institution. Pranks generally consist of decorating the couple's car, often with double entendre graffiti.

FUNERAL CUSTOMS

Until World War Two, funeral homes were few in the Ozarks and, except in the larger towns, embalming was not practiced. This meant that people had to be buried very soon after death. Most communities had at least one person who made coffins, which were generally plain boxes of pine or other woods locally available. These casketmakers sometimes acquired reputations for being odd, or even sinister, as was the case with the protagonist of the following story, which is found in *Ghost Stories from the American South*:

Well, Ashberry—we called him Rip—made caskets for all the local townsfolk. He did this for over fifty years—actually more than that if you count his father. A doctor moved in one day, where Rayburn lives now, but was so scared—this was in 1924 or thereabouts—he moved out. Well, this old casketmaker seemed always his happiest when death was in the air. He would look you up and down when he saw you—made you feel kind of crazy. The oddest thing about this old man was that he made his own casket and prided himself on this fact and would even show people when they had a death in the family. Well, he had a call for a child's casket and set to work on it, but before it was ever finished he disappeared. The people believed he would always return. During the stormiest part of a storm you can hear him at work trying to finish out his work. I tell kids if they ain't good, he will build them a casket. (pp. 64–65)

Preparing a body for burial was done by relatives and neighbors of the deceased, rarely by immediate family members. The corpse was washed thoroughly and dressed in a nice suit or dress. On rare occasions a person who was not dead but was in a comatose state was prepared for burial. This is what happened in the following two narratives, the second of which is merely told for humor:

Back in the thirties they didn't have any funeral homes around here. When somebody died the people in the community prepared them for burial, usually somebody who had some experience in that line, you know. I mean there were people who knew how to take care of the corpse after a person died and they did it a lot of the time when someone died. Of course, there probably wasn't a lot of people too eager to do that job anyway. Well, anyhow, the schoolteacher down here his first wife died, or everyone thought she did. Well, she was laid out and people were sitting up with her and she started sitting up in her casket. It scared everyone pretty bad, but then they realized that she hadn't been dead, she was just in a trance, or something, and people thought she was dead. After so long a period she came out of it and sat up. It's a good thing there weren't any real undertakers around here then because if they had got hold of her she would have been dead, sure enough. When they embalm them they fix them up so they are dead for sure. That woman lived eight more years but when she died the next time she really was dead. The second time she didn't get up out of her casket.[1]

There's a woman they thought she's dead and they started to the graveyard with her, they started into the gate with her; and the wagon wheel hit a post, and jarred the wagon, and she come to. She lived a long time after that and she died and they started back through the gate with her, and the old man said to be careful and don't hit the post again.[2]

One former practice that was taken seriously was staying up all night with a dead person. This custom figures in the following narrative, a version of a tale that is always told as a true experience rather than as a funny, but fictitious, story:

A bunch of them boys—and they was pretty rough and tough, you see. An old man, an old German, an old bachelor, lived back in there and he got sick and he died. They set up with them until they buried 'em back then. These two guys was setting up with this old man. They was in an old log cabin. And this old German he raised a whole bunch of sweet potatoes. He had a whole bunch of 'em there, see. They got hungry and there was an old fireplace, they had a fire in there. They was roasting them potatoes in that fireplace. They got 'em roasted and they was setting there eating 'em. Directly one of 'em said, "That damned ol' devil, if he knowed we was eating his sweet potatoes he'd come alive."
Directly one of 'em looked around and he rared up. And they say, boy, they hit the door and one of 'em run into the face of the door, a little ol' low door. Knocked him out and that one grabbed him up across the shoulder and they run off and went off, finally found somebody to go back with 'em and said they told him that old man come alive up there. Said he was sitting up in the bed. When they got back up there and started checking and when they laid him out his toes had got under that metal rail across the foot of the bed and his leaders had drawed and pulled him up there. They wouldn't go back until they got somebody to go back with 'em. They was supposed to be rough and tough.[3]

At present, the practice of staying up all night has been modified considerably. Generally, the family establishes visiting hours at the funeral home, and most friends stop by to view the corpse and visit with the family. A few very close friends may spend some more time with the family at home. Neighbors, often members of the family's home church, provide food for the immediate family and their relatives for two to three days, including time both before and after the funeral.
The funeral itself is usually very brief, the ceremony consisting of about thirty minutes in the church and an even briefer graveside ceremony. Although family preferences dictate these matters, in most instances the casket is open before the funeral starts, then closed and opened again for viewing at the end of the church service. Generally, the casket is not opened again at graveside.

REVIVALS

One of the most persistent customs having nothing to do with the life cycle or with holidays is the revival. Most Protestant denominations hold a revival, or "protracted meeting," once a year. These events have their origins in the Great Revival of 1800, when churches—Methodist, Baptist, and Presbyterian—faced the problem of keeping pace with a rapidly expanding population by creating two new practices. One of these was circuit riding, in which a minister traveled on horseback over a regular circuit to preach to the people. The second was the camp meeting, when many people gathered outdoors to listen to preaching over an extended period of time. For several years camp meetings drew enormous crowds, with one Kentucky meeting being said to have attracted twenty-five thousand people. As late as 1837 Charles Fenton Mercer Noland said that ten thousand people attended a northern Arkansas camp meeting.

Although revivals are held almost exclusively in churches, in an earlier day they took place in the schoolhouse, lodge hall, or whatever building was then being used by the church. They were also held in tents and in "brush arbors," open-air places sheltered by an arch of trees and foliage. Joe Cranfield, a resident of Kissee Mills, Missouri, explains how these brush arbors were constructed: "The men would go out and hunt a place out in the woods, . . . and they'd cut poles and forks and build a scaffold up overhead there and then they'd cover that with brush for shade. I've seen as much as an acre covered that way" (in *Ozark Baptizings*,

Brush arbor held by Church of Christ, Brandsville, Missouri (Photo courtesy *The Ozarks Mountaineer*)

ONCE COMMON IN BIBLE BELT—Brusharbor meetings were once a common sight in the Bible Belt area of the

speaker at the meeting which concludes Saturday night. Services are at 8 p.m. nightly. The public is being welcomed

Hangings, and Other Diversions, p. 81). Shade was important, because revivals, particularly those held in open air, usually happened in July or August, a time of year that was generally very warm and sunny.

Baptism in southern Missouri (Photo courtesy *The Ozarks Mountaineer*)

Today, one minister is usually in charge of a revival, but in nineteenth-century camp meetings it was not uncommon for several preachers to take part. The style of preaching then, as now, tended to be of the "hell fire and brimstone" type, heavy on emotion and light on subtlety. This dramatic style is discussed by Joseph Nelson, who spent some time in the 1940s teaching near the Missouri-Arkansas border. He notes that one revival minister "carried us back to the Flood, running across the rostrum to pound on the wall (the door of the Ark) as he screamed, 'Noe-y, let me in! Let me in!' But Noah refused to hear his plea. He dropped to his knees, fighting the raging waters around him, and then, arms wide, still on his knees, he made the plea that all who were not uneasy for their souls come knock at the Ark to which Jesus would gladly admit us" (in *Backwoods Teacher*, p. 148).

Testimonies remain an important feature of revivals because they lead to conversions, and the more conversions the greater the revival's success. Few testimonies are as successful as the one described in the following account. At this Missouri revival the testimony started a half hour before preaching was slated to begin:

> There was an old lady got up from Arkansas. She started in. She said, "When I first went to Arkansas, there was no Christians down there that I knowed of but myself." Says, "I finally got acquainted with a neighbor woman, a Christian. She belonged to my church." Says, "We'd get out and meet in the woods and have prayers. That was about all we could do, and kiss each other when we'd separate." . . . She says, "And it was like pulling water over a pulley. We could feel that spirit come down."
>
> That thing broke loose, and they got that testimony meetin' started, and it lasted till after two o'clock, and they was thirteen conversions came out of that testimony. The preacher couldn't do nothing with 'em. He tried to stop them, but they wasn't nothing' doin'. They was testifyin' all over that place (in *Ozark Baptizings*, pp. 83–84).

Although revivals continue in full force, the brush arbors and large open-air meetings are, for all practical purposes, a thing of the past. Indeed, few of today's worshippers have even seen a brush arbor, much less attended a meeting at one.

New Year's Day and Old Christmas

Two calendar customs in January, New Year's Day and Old Christmas, were traditionally observed, although that is no longer true of the latter. January 1 is ushered in with firecrackers and general noisemaking, and people eat black-eyed peas or hoppin John, a dish made of hog jowls and black-eyed peas. The origin of this food custom seems to be unknown, but some people believe that it will bring them luck throughout the year. Others, of course, partake in the tradition just because it is a tradition. Still others believe there is some historical basis for the practice:

> Mr. Walter Ridgeway, of West Plains, Missouri, always contended that this custom began in Civil War days; some planters who had nothing to eat but black-eyed peas at a New Year's dinner were lucky enough to regain their fortunes, and later on they somehow connected this good luck with the New Year's hoppinjohn. Other hillfolk, however, have told me that the custom of eating black-eyed peas on New Year's is much older than the War between the States (in *Ozark Magic and Folklore*, p. 80).

In the nineteenth and twentieth centuries, many Ozarkers took seriously the belief that if you opened your windows for a few minutes on New Year's Eve, just before midnight, bad luck would go out and good luck would come in. While this tradition was still practiced well into the mid-twentieth century, it was increasingly done more just because it always had been than because of any belief in its efficacy.

Old Christmas, January 6, is also known as "Green Christmas" or "Twelfth Night." In pioneer days this date for the celebration of Christ's birth was more popular than December 25. It was said that on January 5, the eve of Old Christmas, cattle would kneel down and bellow exactly at midnight, and, according to some, the animals had the gift of speech on this night. But by the twentieth century most Ozarkers considered this a tradition that only uneducated or naive people adhered to. In 1922 a McDonald County, Missouri, farmer told the following to Vance Randolph as a true story:

One time there was a little boy lived away back in the hills. His paw and maw was good Christian folks, but kind of old-fashioned. They told him that Christmas comes on the sixth of January, and on Christmas Eve the cattle fall down on their knees at midnight. And they said the cows could talk that night, just like people.

Well, everybody knows Christmas used to come several days later than it does now; some of them old settlers still have their Christmas in January, and they call it Old Christmas. That's a history, and you can't get around history. But it ain't likely that the cattle are going to kneel down at midnight, because a cow don't know nothing about religion, and how could they remember what day it is, anyhow? Still, you got to admit that cattle can kneel down whenever they feel like it, so it might be the notion would hit 'em all at once on Christmas Eve. But we all know in reason that cows can't talk, because it is against nature. Them old folks didn't have no education, and they believed all kind of things that people don't take any stock in nowadays. So they told their little boy about it, and he thought they was telling the truth.

Well sir, when it come the fifth of January, nineteen hundred and four, that little boy never went to sleep because he wanted to hear the cows talk. And when the clock says a quarter to twelve he got up easy, and put on his clothes. And when the clock says ten minutes to twelve he unbarred the door. The old folks was sound asleep, as he could hear them a-snoring like somebody sawing gourds. The little boy stayed out at the barn quite a while, and when he got back to the house the clock says twenty minutes to one. The little boy barred the door again, and took off his clothes, and crawled back in bed. The old folks was still a-snoring. The boy never let on, but he knowed his paw and maw was both liars. And he didn't believe nothing they told him after that.

The folks made the little boy go to church every Sunday, but he figured everything the preacher said was a lie, just like that whopper about the cows talking on Christmas Eve. They kept telling him every boy ought to learn how to read and write, but he thought that was a lie too, and run away from school every chance he got. His paw told him not to fool with them white trash gals that lived up the creek, but he done it anyhow. And by the time he was fourteen years old that boy run off to Oklahoma. Near as the folks could find out, he just hung around gambling halls and whorehouses. Finally he shot a deputy marshal and it looked like they was going to hang him, so he went to Texas and nobody knows what become of him after that.

The church people never could figure out how come that boy to go wrong, but the truth is the whole thing started when his paw and maw told him that fool tale about the cows a-talking. From that time on he thought all the folks was goddam liars, and he didn't believe nothing anybody said. It just goes to show that you got to be careful what you say to little boys, because they take everything mighty serious. It's different with little girls, of course. Girls are a lot smarter than boys, and they don't pay no attention to their paw and maw, anyhow (in *Sticks in the Knapsack and Other Ozark Folk Tales*, pp. 48–49).

DECORATION DAY

Shortly after the Civil War, in 1868, a calendar custom arose that was to become very popular in the Ozarks. It was named Decoration Day because it was to be a day on which graves would be decorated. Initially set on May 30 or the nearest Sunday to it, it came to be observed on various dates ranging from early May to the middle of August and sometimes on a Monday. The following accounts give a good idea of the activities at representative Decoration Day programs. The first appeared in the Marshall, Arkansas, *Mountain Wave* on July 12, 1894:

After leaving town, last Sunday morning we had the pleasure of attending the exercises of the Canaan grave yard decoration, and of all the ceremonies we have ever attended, we think this one was the most imposing and impressive. The crowd assembled at the Shilo church house, 1/2 mile from the cemetery, where the procession of 800 people formed and marched to the cemetery. The procession was headed by a committee on decoration, which consisted of eight young ladies all dressed in deep mourning. When the decoration was done there were several speeches made; three by some little girls, and Messrs. Tenison, Aday, Ferguson and Pate, all made impressive and interesting speeches.

When speaking was over the procession reformed and marched back to the church house where a splendid dinner was spread.

Everything was carried on in the best of order. The crowd was orderly; the speaking was good and the singing was excellent and appropriate.

The people around Canaan are to be congratulated for having the nicest cemetery in the country.

We believe there were not less than 1000 souls in attendance, and think all should feel proud to know that the people would meet at least once a year to pay tribute to our memory, and lay flowers on our tombs (in *Shootin's*, p. 242).

The following appeared in the *Mountain Wave* on May 20, 1898:

Reno Post No. 89, G. A. R., domiciled at Witt Springs, Searcy County, Arkansas, will observe Decoration day, which will be Monday, the 30th of May, 1898. All persons who have friends and relatives buried in the Witt Springs cemetery are expected to be present and take part in the ceremonies and all who will, whether or not they have friends or relatives buried there are invited to be present and take part in the same. All persons are requested to come and bring a basket well filled with grub, so we can have a good time. As this is done under the auspices of the G. A. R. the ex-confederates must not think themselves slighted. They are also invited to come and take part in the same. We expect to have divine services, so preachers of the gospel of all denominations are invited, and more especially the candidates for representative. We expect to have singing, so the musicians are invited to come. We also invite the children to come, especially the Sunday school class.

All persons who come are expected to leave their prejudices and dogs at home and all to come, and whosoever will let them come and don't forget the basket of grub. We promise those who come that there will be good order kept during the day. Come out and let us have a good time and pay our respects to our departed friends.

The program is as follows:

1. The Grand Army will meet at the post room and form a procession and march to the cemetery. All persons present are expected in the procession according as the committee will assign them.

2. At the cemetery we will have divine services.

3. After services the graves of the old soldiers will be decorated by the members of the Post.

4. All graves in the cemetery will be decorated by a committee of young ladies.

5. All persons that have special flowers for special graves will then be permitted to deposit them.

6. Procession will form and march to some suitable place, where dinner will be served.

7. Immediately after dinner we will assemble for speaking.

8. Speaking that will be appropriate for the occasion.

9. Children that have pieces will be permitted to speak them. We will have singing also.

Come out, friends, and let us have a good time, and if you do not enjoy yourself it will be your own fault, and if you do not get plenty to eat it will be because your basket was not full enough (in *Shootin's Obituaries, Politics*, pp. 243–244).

Also in the *Mountain Wave*, on August 19, 1898, was the following article:

The decoration services at the Canaan cemetery, which occurred last Sunday, were both interesting and impressive. The day was fine, though somewhat warm, but the heat did not deter the good people of that vicinity gathering to do honor to departed relatives and friends. About nine hundred people were present.

Bro. Wilcox opened the services with an earnest prayer that was appropriate to the occasion. As the speakers selected failed to make their appearance, Bro. T. M. Ferguson was called upon to address the people, which he did in his usual forceful though kindly manner, and at the conclusion tears were coursing down the cheeks of many of his listeners, and all felt well repaid for having been present to hear such an able address.

Special praise is due to the band of little girls who acted as decorators. They were all dressed in white, and as they hovered over the graves, performing their kindly mission, they appeared like seraphs from the celestial kingdom, they looked so sweet and happy.

The singing class did splendidly, and altogether the decoration services at Canaan was a complete success and much good was accomplished (in *Shootin's*, 244).

Decoration activities are still popular with rural churches, but they no longer attract crowds comparable to those reported in the 1890s.

JULY 4

Most Americans consider July 4 a special holiday because it celebrates the country's freedom from foreign rule, and people who live in the Ozarks are no exception. While no specific activities are associated with this holiday, Silas Turnbo's memories of a Fourth of July celebration in Forsyth, Missouri, provides evidence that some Ozark celebrations are quite memorable:

It has been many years since my first visit to Forsyth, Taney County, Missouri. It was then quite a small village but it did not lack for lively and stirring scenes. The memory of the Fourth of July, 1848, has never faded from my mind, but time and humanity since then have wrought a great change.

The weather was warm and serene, there was not a cloud hardly visible. The citizens of the village and the surrounding country gave a big dinner. It was an old fashioned barbecue and good order prevailed throughout the day. Though the country was thinly settled, yet the size of the crowd that collected on that day was astonishing. They came from far and near and from every direction. Some of the men and women came over fifty miles. The number of people was estimated at 1,500 including children. This was remarkable when we take into consideration the manner of traveling. Some came on horseback, some in ox wagons and hundreds came on foot.

They were all patriotic and enthusiastic and took that occasion to celebrate the great victories by the daring and valor of the American troops in the Mexican War. Peace had already been declared but news could not fly over the world in a minute in those days and the people of Taney County had not learned of the fact, and so they organized a company of volunteers to send to the front. News of the declaration of peace reached Forsyth soon afterward and the company was soon disbanded.

I am not exaggerating when I say that Forsyth was honored on that fourth day of July by the presence of 500 ladies. I was only four years old then, but I never will forget as long as I live what a beautiful appearance the ladies presented as they marched to the table in proper order. Nearly all of them were neatly dressed in clothes of their own manufacture dyed with old fashioned indigo and madder and barks, roots and weeds gathered in the forest. Many of them wore moccasins and had on garbs of dressed buck skins, but a majority of the men and boys wore garments spun and woven by the industrious housewives and daughters. Nearly all the women and girls wore paste board and cedar split bonnets. There were no lemonade stands for speculation nor dancing floors to mar the feeling of those religiously inclined. It was simply an old time gathering of the people with plenty to eat and free to all that were present (in *Turnbo's Tales of the Ozarks*, p. 149).

CHRISTMAS CUSTOMS

Until World War Two it was unusual for Ozark residents to have Christmas trees in their homes. Instead, they participated in a community event commonly called the Christmas Tree, described by May Kennedy McCord in her article "Our Ozark Christmas Days of Long Ago" as "the greatest and most thrilling event of the year" (in *Ozark Mountaineer*, December 1953, p. 10). The tree was decorated with tinsel, popcorn, cranberries, and lighted candles. Often those in attendance were quite impressed by the sight, as was one editor of the *Ozark County News* (December 28, 1893) who wrote about the Christmas tree at Gainesville, Missouri, that "its dazzling beauty and splendor as it met the gaze and admiration of thousands of eyes was something never to be forgotten" (in *Ozark Baptizings*, p. 151).

That the Christmas Tree programs were not casual celebrations is indicated by the schedule slated for Marshall, Arkansas, in 1893 and published in *The Marshall Republican*:

PROGRAMME FOR CHRISTMAS TREE.

To be at the church house on the night of the 25th inst.

COMMITTEES.

On Programme:—Misses Ida Hopper and Mollie Greenhaw, Albert Arnold and W. T. Mitchell.

On Arrangements.—E. W. Gray, P. O. McEntire, W. W. Hale, W. R. Nelson, H. H. Acree, A. Y. Burr, J. C. Hollis, Albert McBride.

On Dressing Tree.—Mrs. V. C. Bratton, Mrs. Henley, Mrs. Redwine, Misses Allie Sanders, Martha Gray, Florence Watts, Nora Lindsey, Sallie Bratton and Laura Sweeny, Dr. Daniel, J. A. Dugger, J. W. Stephenson.

On Decoration.—Lillie Treece, Mattie McBride, Allie Sanders, Nellie Brown, Martha Gray, Emma Wheelock, Mattie Thomas, Josie Stephenson, Mollie Green- haw, Ida Hopper, S. E. Hollabaugh, Wayne Hensley, G. B. Greenhaw, Monroe Sanders, Maude Arnold, Etta Russell and Callie Sanders.

On handing off Presents.—M. A. Sanders, A. Wellborn, S. E. Hollabaugh.

On calling names.—J. F. Henley.

On Delivering Present.—Myrtle Greenhaw, Dottie Robertson, Ero Harvey, Hugh Treece, Flora Phillips and Flavel Redwine.

Santa Claus.———

Floor Manager.—W. P. Hodge.

Ushers.—Berry Bratton, J. T. Gray.

Recitations.—Rilla Hays, Nora Byrd, Cora Hollis, Cora Horn.

Speeches.—W. R. Nelson, Prof. Blankinship, Ulysses S. Bratton and J. M. McCall (in *Shootin's*, p. 236).

Gifts for adults and children alike were placed under the tree, and while certain people were selected to take charge of distributing presents, the entire audience really participated in handing out gifts. The following report appeared in the *Christian County Republican* in January 1903:

As each beautiful doll was taken up from the tree each little girl waited with eager expectation to hear her name called, or when a beautiful album or picture was handed down the young ladies would wait with blushing cheek to know if they had been remembered by their sweetheart, and when the drums or guns were held up each small boy looked with eager eye to see if his name was on the tag. And the eyes of those whose heads were frosted over by the frosts of many winters twinkled with delight when their names were called (in *Ozark Baptizings*, p. 151).

In addition to regular presents, in most communities gag gifts would be hung from limbs of the tree. For example, a newly married couple might be given a diaper, or a large slab of ham might be given a town's best known Seventh-Day Adventist. Local merchants contributed to a fund to insure that every child would receive a present, and collections were taken up for special gifts, such as a suit of clothes for a local minister.

Most people enjoyed the Christmas Tree immensely, but there were those who disapproved of the custom. In a 1908 letter to the editor of the *Ash Grove Commonwealth* in Missouri, a writer condemned them as "Puritanical, intolerant, and Pharisaical" (in *Ozark Baptizings*, p. 152). Sometimes presents were distributed not from a tree but from some other decorative device, such as a snow house, an arch, a windmill, or an old log church.

While most communities still have a Christmas tree, usually on the courthouse square, few have the Christmas Tree programs; those had mostly disappeared by 1950. What remains in the present day are private, home Christmas programs. These generally consist of singing and even recitations, with people occasionally writing special poems. Often, these are humorous in intent, as was the parody written by Thomas Sherman for his own family's Christmas programs in Stone County, Arkansas:

THE NIGHT BEFORE CHRISTMAS
(with apologies to Clement Moore)

'Twas the night before Christmas and all through the shack,
The snow was drifting in through a crack.
The stockings were hung on nails in a row:
And every sock had a hole through the toe.
The children were restless, worried and jumpy;
Because the mattress was worn out—and lumpy.
And Ma in her kerchief—and I with bare feet;
Had gone to the kitchen for something to eat.
When out on the lawn there arose a great clatter;
And I was most positive, what was the matter.
Away to the window I flew in a spurt.
(Stubbed my big toe; and, oh my, how it hurt!)
The moon, on the breast of the new-fallen snow;
Showed a familiar figure below.
For, who to my wandering eyes should appear?
But, Father; coming home loaded with beer.
He slipped on the ice which had gotten quite slick;
And lit on the ground like a truck-load of brick.
More rapid than eagles his curses they came:
And he whistled and shouted, and called them by name.
"Now dash it! Now damn it! This ice is sure risky!
And I have just busted an armload of whiskey."
To the edge of the porch, he crawled on his knees;
And pulled himself up the steps by degrees.
At the top of the steps, I then heard him call!
And knew, that, again he was starting to fall.
As dry leaves before the wild hurricane fly,
He lit on his neck with his feet toward the sky.

So, up to the house-top the curses they flew.
We could sure hear them: the neighbors did, too!
And then in a twinkling I heard a loud scratch;
As he tried to get his key into the latch.
When I turned from the window and looked toward the door;
He shoved it open and fell on the floor.
His clothes were all soaking—and so were his feet!
And his trousers they had a big hole in the seat.
His coat was a mess, where he fell on his back:
And I knew he was carrying all he could pack.
His eyes they were wrinkled—and he looked quite scary:
His nose it was almost as red as a cherry.
His droll little mouth was drawn up in a bow:
(Because he had lost his false teeth in the snow.)
The stump of a pipe he held tight in his hand:
And the odor was something quite hard to withstand.
He had a broad face and a little round tummy;
That he had acquired—'cause he was a rummy.
He was chubby and plump—a quite silly old coot;
That Mother had many times threatened to shoot.
When he loosened his tie—and pulled down the spread;
It gave me to know he was going to bed.
He spoke not a word—but went straight to his work;
And pulled off his shoes and his socks with a jerk!
And only excluding his shoes and his hose,
He climbed into bed with all of his clothes.
He started to snore—it was sort of a whistle;
and Ma hit him once with a quite heavy missile!
But, I heard him exclaim as Ma turned out the light,
"Happy Christmas to all—though I'm just a bit tight!"[4]

FOLK MEDICINE

Until the post–World War Two era, trained physicians were few in number in the Ozarks, and those were found mainly in towns. This meant that most Ozarkers either had to rely on their own resources or to use doctors that most people openly referred to as "quacks." This appellation, however, did not mean that such practitioners were regarded as incompetent or frauds, merely that they had no formal training. Actually, occupying the niche between regular physicians and the application of home remedies, there were "chills-an'-fever doctors," "power doctors," and "yarb doctors" or "nature doctors." The chills-an'-fever doctors usually had some formal medical training, although some merely "picked up doc-toring" by working with a physician whose practice they eventually in-herited. Such doctors were welcomed by the medical profession, which often advised them.

Dr. Silas S. Stacy, who lived several years in Isabella, Missouri, seems to have been something in between a regular physician and a chills-an'-fever doctor:

He was a prominent practitioner of medicine and he rode over part of Ozark County and the edge of some of the adjoining counties dealing out medicine to the sick. Stacy was a reformer in the art of medicine and in the main followed the rule of the Eclectic school of medicine. He was the first physician as far as I know that introduced a mild form of treatment of the sick on Ozark County. He was a close student of the study of diseases and their treatment. He knew but little about medical colleges and diplomas. He was a great admirer of John M. Scudder, M. D., of Cincinnati, Ohio, who advocated the use of special remedies for special condi-tions of disease and not the names. He held out that man changed the name of diseases which was misleading. He claimed that physicians would have better success with the ailments of humanity if they would leave off the so-called names of diseases and strike at the cause of complaint and not the symptoms (in *Turnbo's Tales of the Ozarks*, p. 30).

The chills-an'-fever doctors of yesteryear have disappeared, but the power doctors and the yarb, or nature, doctors are still very active. The power doctors claim no scientific knowledge but use charms, spells, pray-ers, and various types of magic in their healing efforts. Believing that they have supernatural abilities to cure certain specific ailments, they rarely attempt any general practice. Usually they do not take money for their services, although occasionally they will accept or even demand valuable presents. These practitioners are frequently elderly women who, accord-ing to many people, have the ability to cool fevers merely by the laying on of hands, or to draw fire from burns by blowing upon the inflamed areas, or to stop bleeding by using formulaic charms. Usually, the power doctors have to see the person they are treating, but as Mrs. M. R. Smith of Mationville, Missouri, told May Kennedy McCord, even that is not always a prerequisite:

Speaking of stopping blood, I can do it. I have on several occasions. My mother had cancer of the face, and it would bleed till she would almost pass on. So my brother-in-law told us about an old man in the neighborhood who could stop blood, and all he needed was to be told—did not have to see the person. So we sent him word one day and the blood just stopped, all at once. Why or how you will have to decide for yourself, but it did stop (in *Ozark Magic and Folklore*, p. 124).

While power doctors guard their secrets closely, they are not averse to sharing their knowledge with interested parties; however, specific rules apply to this giving of information. Some say it can only be passed on to persons of the opposite sex, while others maintain it must only be given to members of the same sex. This esoteric knowledge is transmitted orally, since most power doctors feel that they will lose their abilities if their lore is written down or published. They are also particular about whom they will work on and will not usually try to help a person who does not have a strong belief in their abilities. Although many people view the power doctors as ignorant purveyors of mumbo jumbo, a surprisingly large number swear to their ability to get miraculous results that would not be achieved by conventional doctors.

Most people now consider yarb, or nature, doctors merely an alternative to regular physicians, rather than their first choice for medical treatment. Nevertheless, there are still some who seek the yarb doctors out first and who refuse to have anything to do with conventional physicians. These persons consider the natural treatments superior to drugs prescribed by AMA physicians.

Yarb doctors rely heavily on the healing properties of herbs, barks, roots, and the like. For internal use, tea is made from these substances and the patient is given hefty doses of the liquid. Nature doctors are also strong believers in poultices that are applied both hot and cold for a variety of ailments. Even some trained physicians admit that much of the yarb doctors' treatment has some validity and that there is a great deal about sickness and healing that medical science cannot yet explain. Yet not even the staunchest believer in these remedies believe that they always work. Zora Arbaugh Moore of Ozone Mountain, Arkansas, recalled that a relative, Belle Arbaugh, "killed one of her kids on turpentine. She just kept giving it to him and giving it to him, and that stuff killed him."[5] (At the same time, few trained doctors would maintain that their cures work 100 percent of the time.)

Many people prefer to forego the services of any doctor, trained or otherwise, opting to treat themselves. This is particularly true when the ailments aren't considered major. In these instances people tend to use the same remedies that the nature doctors do. Honey, for example, is thought to cure a variety of complaints ranging from muscle cramps to bed-wetting. It is particularly easy to use with children because it tastes good. In some instances honey probably acts as a placebo and works only because the person taking it believes it will work. That is probably the case when muscle cramps are cured with two teaspoonfuls of honey given to the patient at each meal and then occasionally after the problem disappears in order to prevent its reappearance. The same principle may be at work when insomnia is treated with a teaspoon of honey at supper and then two more teaspoons immediately before retiring. On the other hand, applying honey to the skin over an area that has been severely burned in order to prevent pain and the forming of blisters, as well as curing bed-wetting in children by giving them a teaspoonful of honey, may have some actual therapeutic value.

Turpentine is still very popular as a folk cure for a variety of ills including snakebite and worms. It is given both internally and externally. For a snakebite the usual treatment is to rub turpentine on it, the assumption being that the turpentine will draw the poison out of the body. To purge worms, however, turpentine has to be taken internally, often in large doses. This cure is, in some instances, worse than the problem being treated, particularly when administered to small children. While the turpentine may eliminate worms, heavy doses of it have a detrimental effect on the kidneys. Still, as one woman said, "All the old people used turpentine. I've took turpentine lots of times. Why just a drop is good for cramps or stuff like that."[6] Moderation, then, is the key.

There are various remedies for drawing out infection resulting from mishaps such as a nail in the foot. One is to put the foot in a liquid made from boiling the pink blossoms of smart weed. Another is to make a poultice of hot ashes and water and place it on the infected part. Practitioners of these remedies frequently have success stories to tell about the efficacy of these treatments, of which the following is representative: "One time, when Grandpa and Nanny were first married, a little 7-year-old girl named Goldie was staying with them. Goldie had an infection in her toe and hot, red streaks were running up her leg. Nanny thought she was going to die with gangrene until Great-grandpa Hignite told her to just go out in the woods, get a May apple, cut a hole in it and put it over the big toe. That drew out the 'pison' and cured it."[7]

There are many home remedies for taking care of burns. Treatment with honey has already been mentioned; another is a mixture of witch hazel and meat grease. The following anecdote describes one remedy for a fresh cut: "Once when Uncle Bud stepped on a broken cup handle and cut his toe completely off, Grandpa had him put his foot in kerosene and wrap rags around the toe and it grew back on as good as new."[8]

Sassafras and ginseng teas are both considered very useful, the former for thinning the blood and the latter for digestion and "sinaka" (sciatica). Ginseng is also thought to extend life and to strengthen sexual power in men; while both these beliefs are held in various parts of the world, there is no recognized scientific validity to either claim. Ginseng does contain some B vitamins, and Russian and Chinese scientists claim to have isolated substances in the root that influence cardiovascular functions. These claims are not generally accepted in the West, and the scientific procedures that gave rise to them have not been duplicated here either.

Tonics made from poke roots, burdock, mullein, yellowroot, and powdered rhubarb are taken in the winter in lieu of vitamins. Spicewood tea was once popular and is still used occasionally for "breaking the measles out." "Up on the mountain where I lived, it grows. There was a lot of it. It smells good. You just pick it up and make a tea out of it, like a catnip tea or something like that. It's a kind of a bush. You break the little limbs and make tea out of it. Yeah, you sweeten it. If you didn't sweeten it, it would taste horrible."[9]

Mullein root combined with two tablespoons of honey and one-half teaspoon of alum was one popular recipe for homemade cough syrup; another was made when wild cherry bark and sugar were boiled in water to which was added two spoons of brandy. These once commonly used concoctions are rarely made now, because it is easier to buy cough syrup at a drug store. "You couldn't run to the drugstore and get this and that like you can now. They just had to make out with what they had."[10]

CHAPTER 5

Ozark and Appalachian Folk Music

The folk music found in the Ozarks would seem to indicate that, culturally speaking, the area is Appalachia West. In matters of repertoire and instrumentation, the folk traditions of the two mountain regions are very similar. Even the methods of instrument-playing are alike. For example, one of the prominent guitar-playing techniques in the Ozarks is known as "Carter style," after Maybelle Carter, the Appalachian country musician who was its most influential proponent. In this approach, the guitarist picks a melody line with the thumb of the right hand while brushing the index finger of the right hand across the strings to sound the harmonic accompaniment. In both regions this method of guitar playing has been overshadowed in recent years by the "Travis style," in which a guitarist picks out a melody line with the fingers of the right hand while using the thumb of the right hand to strike the bass notes. Although very popular in Appalachia and the Ozarks, this style actually originated in western Kentucky.

Because there are so many similarities between Appalachian and Ozark folk music and song, most authorities have assumed they are exactly the same. During the past two decades, a few observers have noted that there are some differences as well, though some of these do not hold up under investigation. One observation is that Ozark folk music has been more isolated from popular music influences—jazz, vaudeville, and Tin Pan Alley—than has the folk music of other regions of the United States. But any brief search through an Ozark collection such as Vance Randolph's *Ozark Folksongs* will easily disprove this statement. Although there are many Child ballads and similar items of some antiquity, there are also songs such as Gussie L. Davis's "The Fatal Wedding," George "Honey Boy" Evans's "Down in Arkansaw," Hoyt "Slim" Bryant's "Mother, the Queen of My Heart," and Billy Hill's "Little Box of Pine on the 7:29" that are taken from Tin Pan Alley or commercial country music sources. Their presence provides ample evidence that Ozark folk musicians did not live in a world shut off from the influence of popular culture; thus, this folk music is not "purer" than that found in other parts of the United States. It has also been suggested that Ozark folk music is more modal than that found elsewhere in North America, but, if this is so, it has not been demonstrated and is not provable on the basis of what is currently known about American folk music.

Linda Burman-Hall's characterization of Ozark fiddle music as a distinctive style is less easy to dismiss, because it is based on analysis of field-collected data and is not merely speculative or wishful. She says that some of the chief distinctions between Appalachian and Ozark fiddle styles are that Ozark musicians play with a greater variety of tempos, without instrumental adjustment for triple stops, and with frequent use of glissando. Perhaps Burman-Hall is correct, although my own fieldwork in both regions does not support all of her points. Furthermore, since she confined her research to an examination of just two tunes, "Soldier's Joy" and "Bonaparte's Retreat"—even though she had forty-three versions—it seems a bit premature to argue that all of the differences found in such a small sample are in fact characteristic of the fiddle music of the two regions. Finally, Burman-Hall's discussion and all similar ones are on somewhat shaky ground because of the sketchy history of collecting folk music in America. More collecting has been carried out in the southern mountains, both the Appalachians and the Ozarks, than in most other sections of the United States. It is thus possible that features thought to be distinctive aspects of southern mountain folk music may be widespread and actually characteristic of the folk music of other areas, which may not be known simply because the music of these other sections has not received the attention given to the Ozarks and Appalachians.

However, it is still safe to say that there are some features that distinguish Ozark folk music from that found in the mountains to the east. My own fieldwork, as well as that conducted by other folklorists and collectors in both Appalachia and the Ozarks, makes it clear that Ozark folk music is not just a carbon copy of Appalachian folk music, even though the two forms bear great similarities. There are three significant features of Ozark folk music that are not derived from Appalachian sources. First, both instrumentally and vocally, Ozark musicians are more likely to eliminate minor notes and minor sounds. This is, of course, not invariably true, but it is relatively common. Thus, where the following chord ♭ would occur in a song, it would be played in this manner . I once asked a guitarist-singer why she left out the minor sounds in many of the songs she sang, and she professed that she didn't really know but thought the songs sounded better that way. She then added that it was the way most of the people in her community used to perform them, and she guessed that she had simply forgotten that the songs ever had minor sounds. Of course, there are many Ozark folk musicians who have never followed this approach to music.

Second, a sizeable body of Ozark music, although certainly not the dominant one, consists of European-American songs and tunes from groups of non-Anglo-Saxon backgrounds. There is a strong French tradition, including songs such as "The Returned Soldier" and "La Guignolee (La Gaie-Annee)," that has thrived in the Ozarks but has received minimal attention from folklorists. There is also the music of such cultural groups as African-Americans, which has been virtually overlooked by those who have paid attention to Ozark folk music. So little attention has been given to the music of Ozark blacks that it is impossible to speak with authority about the nature of this group's music, but it is certainly an aspect of traditional Ozark music that is not derived from Appalachia. Much the same can be said about the folk music of the many other ethnic and cultural groups found in the Ozarks, most of these people having received no attention from folklorists or folk music enthusiasts.

Third, some of the traditional music found in the Ozarks is indigenous; this is particularly true of ballads. While many of the folk ballads traditional to the Ozarks are the same ones found in Appalachia and other parts of the United States, there are quite a few "event" ballads that originated in the Ozarks and seem to be known nowhere else. The following song, "The Iron Mountain Baby," about a 1902 incident in which a baby was placed in a satchel and thrown off a passenger train operated by the Iron Mountain Railroad, is one example:

The Iron Mountain Baby

I have a song I would like to sing
It's awful but it's true
About a babe thrown from a train
By a mother I know not who.

This little babe but a few days old
Was in a satchel lain
His clothes around it folded
And thrown from the train.

The train was running at full speed
The northbound no. 4
And as they crossed Big River bridge
They cast it from the door.

A mother unkind a father untrue
But this I am bound to say

It must have grieved that mother's heart
To cast her babe away.

They bruised its head and hurt its arm
The fall upon the ground
A kind old man lived on a farm
This poor little baby found.

They washed and bathed its little head
And soon they hushed its cry
May God bless them while they live
God bless them when they die.

This little baby, bless its heart
I cannot tell its name
Now has a mother to take its part
A father just the same.

Come one come all attention give
This lesson is for you
Teach your children how to live
And tell them what to do.

This wicked world is full of sin
God help us all to pray
And be prepared to enter in
The fold on judgment day.

Among the other "event" ballads unique to the Ozarks are "Little Alice Summers," about a small girl who was lost for a brief time in the Missouri Ozarks in the late 1890s, and "Lee Mills," a "goodnight" ballad about an Arkansas robber-murderer that appears later in chapter 5. Although these and other ballads deal with tragedies or events that occurred in the Ozarks, they follow a format typical of "event" ballads found in Appalachia, as well as in other parts of the United States.

MUSICAL INSTRUMENTS

The most important instrument in Ozark folk music is the human voice. One folksinger told me, "If you have a good voice you don't need any other instrument. The guitars and all that are just crutches people use. Anyone with a good, strong voice doesn't need them." Certainly the human voice was around long before any other musical instrument. In the Ozark phenomenon called hootling, the voice is used like an instrument and played off against reed pipes.

Ozark folksingers perform songs in what might be called the objective style. This means that they do not resort to musical gimmicks to call attention to important points in a song and do not allow themselves to intrude on the song's message. Instead, they let the lyrics do the work, acting as the conduit through which the words reach the audience. Unlike pop and art singers, who perform songs, folksingers present songs. They do not call attention to important points in a song by using diminuendos or crescendos. Neither do they broadcast the coming end of a song by using ritardandos. Instead, throughout a song the folksinger holds a steady, consistent tempo, maintaining essentially the same pitch, volume, and timbre. The folksinger also sings in a natural, unaffected style and, of course, sings material from his or her own folk tradition.

After the human voice, the most important instrument in Ozark folk music is the fiddle. It is also known as a violin, but most folk musicians refer to it as a fiddle for the very good reason that there is a difference between the fiddle and the violin. The difference lies in how the instrument is adjusted and how it is played. The violinist deliberately uses an extremely high bridge to prevent double stops (the striking of two strings at a time with the fiddle bow) or triple stops (the striking of three strings at a time). The fiddler makes great use of double and triple stops. Violinists have standard tunings and bowing techniques; fiddlers have tunings and bowings. Most fiddlers use steel strings rather than the gut strings favored by violinists. In some respects, then, fiddling is more complicated and difficult than violin playing.

There were several reasons why the fiddle became so popular in Ozark folk music. One is that it is a small instrument that is easily transported. Another is that it has a good deal of volume, an important consideration in the days before microphones and public address systems. Until relatively recently, most musical instruments in the Ozarks were used mainly to accompany dancing. It was therefore essential to have an instrument that could be easily heard over the crowd.

As is true of most instruments used by Ozark folk musicians, it is unknown exactly when the fiddle was invented. It certainly owes much to instruments that predated it, such as the rebec, Renaissance fiddle, and the *lira da braccio*. The earliest known makers of the instrument were from the towns of Cremona and Brescia in Italy. In one sense the Amati family was the most important family of violin makers, because Nicola Amati taught Antonio Stradivari, the most famous violin maker ever. The instrument made it to the New World by about 1650 and came to the Ozarks with French settlers in the early eighteenth century.

Two popular Ozark fiddle tunes are given on pages 102 and 103.

In the nineteenth century, the five-string banjo became very popular

DEVIL'S DREAM

as an instrument to accompany the fiddle. Popularized by blackface minstrel show performers, the banjo is of African origin, with the earliest reports of it dating from the mid-seventeenth century, at which time it was called the banza or strum-strum. In 1784 Thomas Jefferson, in his *Notes on the State of Virginia*, referred to it as the banjar. The invention of the fifth string, a drone, is often erroneously attributed to Joel Walker Sweeney (1810–1860), the first well-known and widely traveled white banjoist. Although Sweeney did popularize the instrument among urban audiences in the United States and England, the addition of the fifth

COTTON EYED JOE

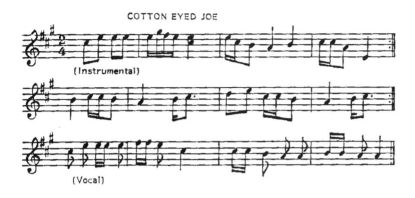

(Instrumental)

(Vocal)

string to the banjo was not his invention. It is known that slaves had banjos with the short string well before Sweeney was born, so it is either an African invention or an African-American one.

There are two methods of playing the banjo, down-stroking and finger-picking. Down-stroking, the style most prominent among minstrel show performers, is the older style. It involves striking down on the strings with the thumb and back (nail) of the index or middle finger, the hand always moving downwards as it hits the strings. Because the hand is held in a shape roughly resembling a claw hammer, this is sometimes called "clawhammer"-style banjo. Other names for this style include frailing, knocking, rapping, and drop thumb.

Finger-picking was first mentioned in an 1865 instruction book by Frank B. Converse, but he credited the Buckley family as the first to play in this style. This became known as "classical" or "classic" banjo style and began replacing the older "stroke" styles in the 1870s when the banjo came to be popular as a genteel parlor instrument for the performance of popular and light classical music. About 1900, finger-picking entered rural folk tradition among black players and white players alike. From these sources both a two-finger (thumb and index finger) and a three-finger (thumb, index finger, and middle finger) style developed. The latter has erroneously become known as "Scruggs style" after Earl Scruggs, a bluegrass musician who is its most famous proponent. This style, which involves a syncopated roll with the fingers picking up on the strings, is the most widely heard style of banjo-playing today, mainly because it is occasionally featured on radio and television, whereas the down-stroking style rarely receives such attention.

An instrument popularly associated with folk music is the six-string guitar. It is, however, one of the most recent arrivals on the scene. Even though guitar-shaped instruments date to 1350 B.C. in the Middle East and the word "guitar" originated in the Middle and Far East (from *guit*, the Arabic word for four, and *tar*, the Sanskrit word for string), the instrument known today is of recent vintage, dating back not more than two centuries. During the nineteenth century the guitar was regarded as a genteel parlor instrument. Only in the twentieth century did the guitar become important in Ozark folk music, being introduced in many sections of the Ozarks by black deckhands on steamboats that plied Ozark rivers. For example, in Stone County, Arkansas, in the southern Ozarks, a steamboat worker recalled only by the name "Nigger Roy" influenced many locals to take up the guitar.

Once the guitar was introduced it caught on very quickly, for two main reasons: it was easy to play, at least in comparison with the fiddle, and it enabled the musician to back up a song by playing chord progressions rather than the melody line as was necessary with the fiddle. The two most popular methods of playing the guitar are plectrum and finger-picking. In one, a plectrum, also called a flat pick, is held in the right hand and used to strike the strings. In the other, the player strikes the strings with several picks on his fingers or plucks them with just his fingers. As we have seen, the two styles of finger-style guitar that are popular in the Ozarks are the "Carter style" and the "Travis style." The Travis style has become the more popular in recent years because it involves a more flexible method of playing. In the Carter style, the guitarist is essentially confined to playing the melody line on the bass strings, using the treble strings for harmony and rhythm.

Although the fiddle, banjo, and guitar are the instruments most frequently used by Ozark folk musicians, many other secondary instruments are used. These include both hammered and mountain dulcimer, autoharp, mandolin, harmonica, and picking bow. Of these, none has been more ballyhooed in recent years than the mountain dulcimer. It has been called everything from an American invention to an instrument that harks back to biblical times. Neither of these claims is true. No one has traced the mountain dulcimer, which is also called the lap dulcimer and Appalachian dulcimer, to a time earlier than the nineteenth century. It clearly is derived from a number of European instruments, such as the German *Scheitholt*, the Norwegian *langeleik*, the Swedish *hummle*, the

Finnish *kanteletar*, and the French *epinette des Vosges*, all of which are somewhat similar in size, shape, and volume. The most immediate direct ancestor is probably the Pennsylvania German zither, although authorities are not in total agreement on this point.

The mountain dulcimer was definitely in the Ozarks by the 1850s; this was very early in the instrument's history because the oldest known mountain dulcimers only date from the 1830s. An estate inventory of a man who died in Marcella, Arkansas, in the late 1850s describes a mountain dulcimer; the man had moved to Arkansas from eastern Tennessee. One Missouri family claims that an ancestor invented the instrument, which he called an Indian walkingstick, about the time of the Civil War. While the instrument was known in the Ozarks in the mid-nineteenth century, it was still relatively rare. Fiddler Art Galbraith (1909–1993) from Springfield, Missouri, said he never saw a mountain dulcimer until the 1960s; many other musicians have made similar comments. The main reason that the mountain dulcimer was so rarely encountered is that it is a very personal instrument. Since it doesn't have great volume, it would not have been used as instruments traditionally were, to accompany dances. Instead, the light, delicate tones of the mountain dulcimer were perfectly suited to accompany one's own singing, and it seems likely that until recently that is mainly how it was used.

The word dulcimer is derived from the Latin word *dulce* and the Greek word *melos*, which together mean "sweet song" or "sweet tune." That word is the only thing the hammered dulcimer and mountain dulcimer have in common. The mountain dulcimer is an elongated instru-

Art Galbraith (1909–1993) and his frequent accompanist, Gordon McCann (Photo courtesy *The Ozarks Mountaineer*)

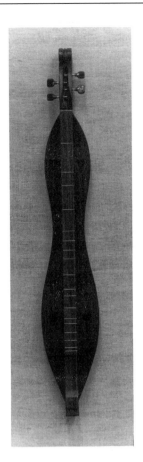

Mountain dulcimer
(Photo courtesy Ozark Folk
Center)

ment, usually with only three or four strings, while the hammered
dulcimer has numerous strings of graduated lengths stretched over a rectangular or trapezoidal box or sounding board. These strings are struck by
two light mallets or hammers held in the hands. Generally regarded as
the ancestor of the piano, this instrument is the one usually referred to
by musicologists and music historians when they speak of the "dulcimer."
Many of the erroneous statements made about the mountain dulcimer are
more accurate when applied to the hammered dulcimer; it would, for
example, be the one that was around in biblical times if any dulcimer
was. It is known by various other names today, including hackbrett and
cimbalom, although in the Ozarks it is most often called a hammered
dulcimer.

   Generally believed to have originated in Persia, in this country the
hammered dulcimer is usually thought of as being used primarily by persons of German ancestry, a view that is at once accurate and misleading.
It is true that the hammered dulcimer is traditional with German-Ameri-

cans, but its use has not been confined to German communities. In the Ozarks at least two hammered dulcimer factories were active in Missouri during the years 1880–1915, one at Neosho and the other at Washington. Unfortunately, these companies' records seem to have disappeared and, to date, efforts to find out anything about their methods of construction and marketing have been fruitless. There were, and still are, also individual craftsmen throughout the Ozarks making hammered dulcimers. Until the 1960s, hammered dulcimer players were far more common in the Ozarks than mountain dulcimer performers. In the past decade the hammered dulcimer has been making a comeback in the region.

The one instrument used by Ozark folk musicians that is of American origin is the autoharp. Indeed, this is one of the few instances in which the name of the inventor is known as well as his motives for creating it. Charles F. Zimmerman, a German immigrant living in Philadelphia in the late nineteenth century, created a new system of music notation. He wanted an instrument on which he could demonstrate his system and didn't think any of those that currently existed were adequate; so he invented his own, or, to be more accurate, he reworked a pre-existing instrument. He took the zither and altered it by adding chord bars which, when pushed by the player, do the fretting automatically.

Perhaps because it was easy to play, the autoharp quickly caught on

Lynn McSpadden and his wife, Mary Katherine, Mountain View, Arkansas. McSpadden is owner of the Dulcimer Shoppe, one of the first mountain dulcimer "factories" in the United States. (Photo courtesy Ozark Folk Center)

with many types of musicians, while Zimmerman's music notation system soon disappeared. Autoharps were sold primarily through mail order houses such as Sears, Roebuck and Montgomery Ward. About 1918 the instrument fell out of favor with everyone but folk musicians, and that is where it has remained ever since. The instrument can be held in a variety of ways, including in the player's lap, or it can be set on a table. Currently most popular in the Ozarks is the method of holding the autoharp in the so-called "Carter style" or "Appalachian style." The latter is the more accurate description, because this style, in which the player holds the autoharp against the left shoulder, probably did originate in southern Appalachia, although it is virtually impossible to prove such an assertion. It is certain, though, that Sara Carter, the Appalachian country musician for whom the style is named, did not invent the method.

For about a century the mandolin has enjoyed some popularity in the Ozarks, although it is as often used as rhythm backup as it is a lead instrument. Originating in Italy in the second half of the eighteenth century, this instrument has four courses of wire strings; it is tuned like a violin and played with a plectrum. There are two styles of mandolins, the "tater bug" and the flat-backed models. The "tater bug" has a deeply vaulted back that is decorated in such a way as to resemble the coloring of the insect commonly called a "tater bug." The flat-back design, which is much more popular today, owes much of its form to the work of Orville Gibson (1856–1918), a Michigan instrument maker for whom the Gibson Guitar Company was named.

Mandolins, like guitars and banjos, were the subject of clubs in American cities in the late nineteenth century, which is when the instrument became known in the Ozarks. Who introduced it to the region or what the circumstances were is unknown. Probably Ozarkers first became aware of the instrument as the result of a mandolin society in one of the region's cities. For the past century it has maintained a steady, if not spectacular, popularity.

Much the same statement can be made about the harmonica, which made its appearance during the first quarter of the nineteenth century. Its sound comes from the so-called "free reed," i.e., a metal tongue fastened over an aperture in a metal frame that vibrates when air pressure is supplied by the player's mouth. Harmonicas are in existence because at the end of the eighteenth century a number of musicians and scientists became interested in the mouth organ of the Far East. The Chinese *sheng* and the Japanese *sho* have histories dating back approximately three thousand years. Today's harmonica is simply a Western variation on these much older instruments.

Since harmonicas have a good deal of volume, they have been used in the Ozarks mainly to accompany dances, although they are also played

Wayne Raney (1921–1993), at left, and Lonnie Glosson, two Ozark musicians who are among the world's best-known harmonica players (Photo from the author's collection)

for one's own listening pleasure. A few Ozark harmonica players have gained national fame, among them Wayne Raney (1921–1993) and Lonnie Glosson, who was born in 1908. Both men specialized in making train sounds, car sounds, and animal sounds of various kinds; although many traditional Ozark harmonica players have such skills, Glosson and Raney developed the techniques further than most of the others.

Raney left a rather detailed account of how and why he took up the harmonica. The role played by chance in his "training" is not unusual in the lives of most modern harmonica players.

When I was still 5 years old, my whole life and plans had to change because they discovered I was born with a rare disease. There was no name for it at that time, but it worked similar to MS that is so common today. It was less severe than MS, but I knew at that point that I had to learn to play some type of music because of the weakness in my legs and feet. Having no money with which to buy guitars and fiddles, I decided to become a harmonica player. My first harmonica was bought by my mother from the sale of eggs that she sold for 5 cents a dozen.

In trying to learn to play the harmonica, I was very lucky to have a one arm hobo stop by our house and say, "My name is Chester Smith can I please have a cold drink of water?" We liked his attitude so well that we invited him to have a meal with us. He told us that his arm was cut off by riding freight trains when he failed to catch one and fell under the train. As he talked on, I found that he was the most outstanding harmonica player under the sun. He is the first person I ever heard that could choke the harmonica making it sound just like a train whistle and all kinds of unusual sounds for those days.

When he learned that I was determined to learn to play the harmonica, he agreed to stay with us and teach me everything he knew. Even at that young age, my belief was that if you had enough faith in God, there was absolutely nothing impossible. The first thing he taught me was to make the train whistle, then after that, all those other unusual sounds began to gradually unfold (in *This Is Wayne Raney*: *"Life Has Not Been a Bed of Roses,"* pp. 5–6).

Without question the oldest instrument used by Ozark folk musicians is the picking bow (or musical bow, as it is sometimes called), a simple, one-string instrument. The player holds the string against the cheek and uses his or her mouth as a resonator, creating different tones by changing the shape of the mouth. The picking bow is believed to be at least thirty thousand years old. It can definitely be dated back seventeen thousand years because on the wall of the cave Les Trois Frères in southwestern France is a painting that has been carbon dated to 15,000 B.C. showing a man playing a picking bow during a musical ceremony. At one point it was assumed that the hunting bow and musical bow had a close relationship. In the late nineteenth century, Henry Balfour concluded that the picking bow was derived from the archer's bow, but some later scholars argued just the opposite. More recently, Curt Sachs offered the theory generally accepted today, which is that the origins of the hunting bow and picking bow are entirely independent of each other. Instead, it seems to be a truncated version of an instrument called the ground zither, or bow. This instrument, which is known in several parts of the world, uses a dug pit as a resonance cavity or sound bowl. A wand is stuck into the

Two picking bow players performing a duet (Photo courtesy Ozark Folk Center)

ground with a string tied to its free end. The other end of the string is knotted into a piece of bark that is placed over the pit and weighted down by a ring of stones or earth. A person standing up creates a melody by altering tension on the string.

While the picking bow is quite ancient and, to some, exotic, it has been known in the Ozarks for at least a century. It is not, however, unique to the Ozarks as is sometimes claimed. Neither has it ever been anything other than a novelty instrument, even though one man told me that it was sometimes used to accompany square dances. He added that this was only done when there were no other instruments available.

FOLK DANCES

Traditionally fiddlers and banjo players performed primarily to accompany dances. Broadly speaking, there are three general types of dances traditional to the Ozarks: solo, couple, and group. The most prominent solo dance performed in the Ozarks is the jig. Although this name was used in the British Isles as long ago as 1500, the Ozark dance is not the same as the British dance. That was characterized by an individual keeping time to music while hopping on one foot and making pointed figures in the air with the other foot. The Ozark jig dance is also a free-style dance, in that there are no set steps. The only requirement is that the dancer keep time to the music while holding a rigid upper body. Some dancers do throw their arms about in a manner reminiscent of shadow boxing, but that is not the norm.

Of the couple dances, the most popular in the Ozarks today are the waltz and the two-step. The waltz, which originated approximately 250 years ago, has a very interesting history. Derived from a German turning dance called the *Ländler*, it was one of the first widely popular dances in which couples faced each other and held each other closely. This feature brought the waltz much criticism, particularly when it reached the United States about 1800. Upon first seeing the dance, President John Tyler described it as very vulgar. Many people considered it a dance that chaste young ladies would not participate in. It was not until the latter half of the nineteenth century that the waltz lost the stigma of being considered lewd and indecent. Now, the three-quarter-time dance is perfectly respectable and is performed on most occasions when there is dancing.

The two-step, a dance requiring two steps per beat, originated later than the waltz. John Philip Sousa's "Washington Post March" (1891) is generally regarded as the number that started the two-step craze. The technique soon became applied to other dances of the period. It remained a pop culture fad for only a short time but persists to the present day as a popular folk dance form. Tunes such as "Joe Turner Blues," "Carroll County Blues," "Florida Blues," and "Faded Love," most of which originally came from commercial music influences, are a few of the favorite Ozark two-step melodies. At one time both the two-step and the waltz were generally thought of as fill-in dances that mainly gave the musicians and dancers a break from square dances. Today, in many cases the opposite is true, with couple dances predominating while square dances are used to break up the routine.

The square dance originated in the early nineteenth century, inspired by contra dances and quadrilles. In the square dance, couples face each other in a square formation, exchanging places in relation to their partners and the other couples. Anti-British feeling at the time of the War of 1812, as well as a need for novelty, resulted in Americans looking to the French for dance styles. An American innovation is the caller outside the square who announces the figures the dancers are to perform. By the 1870s the "singing call" or "patter call" had become commonplace, and it persists today.

Traditionally, dancing, especially square dancing, was viewed unfavorably by many Ozarkers. In Lynn K. McClinton's "The Journal of Arthur Madison Shaw," Shaw, the son of a preacher in Conway, Arkansas, describes the following incident from 1886: "Nobody questioned that dancing was a sin and the remark was often made that it was as great a sin to go to a dance and 'look on' as to dance. My three year old sister and I were constant playmates. One day we were playing some distance from the house in the road. I had on boots. I told her I was going to dance but that it was sinful to 'look on' so she must not watch me! I still remember how dutifully she sat still, looking steadily the other way, while I, dance-devil that I was, performed the heroic act of wickedness" (in *Faulkner Facts and Fiddlings*, pp. 15–16).

A number of arguments were used against dancing: that it led to intemperate behavior, that it was against the will of God, that it was worldly, that it constituted idol worship. Such ideas were expressed in the following letter to the editor in the *Arkansas Gazette*, December 14, 1824:

Though dancing has been practiced from time immemorial, in different ways, expressive of different feelings, such as mirth and jollity, war and bloodshed, yet it has never been a means of expanding the faculties of the human soul, nor of causing the internal beauties of the philosophic mind to bud and bloom and shed their fragrance over the world. It has not helped the fatherless nor the widow in their afflictions, nor been the means of keeping those engaged in it, unspotted from the world. It has never prepared the mind for heavenly meditation, nor for the solemn thought of death and eternal judgement. It has never laid the foundation stone of piety, astronomy, philosophy, usefulness, or greatness, in the world—but its effects have been dreadful on the contrary. It has volatized the human mind. It dissipates the soul, and makes it pleased with wicked company, festivity, and mirth; and disqualifies the mind of the politician for meditation on the welfare of his constituents and the commonwealth. It disorganizes the reflections of the pious as well as the student, and it brings on a train of evil and fatal consequence to young and old.

Many commit a grievous sin before God, by distressing the feelings of their parents and guardians, in frequenting the ballroom, and although they are admonished and entreated with tears to refrain, yet their wicked souls transgress the solemn laws of nature, gratitude, and God, in not submitting to, and honoring their parents, in all things.

Dancing produces late habits: it takes the mind from our studies; it produces a contempt for close application, which only can make the brilliant man. And in lieu of it, produces wicked habits, such as profane swearing, card playing . . . cheating, lying, drinking, which when finished, the unhappy youth graduates with a degree in "Black leg," and thus becomes a nuisance to society. They also spend their time unlawfully by not contributing towards the support of government. . . . The first cash that comes into their hands is appropriated to pay their ball club of their debts of honor. . . . Here injustice to government, to individuals, and dishonesty, together with a misspent life, is the awful result, besides the cursed example they set to those still younger.

But says the objector, shall I have no pleasure in this world? O, yes: the pleasing reflection that you have wiped the tear from the widow's cheek, allayed the orphan's cries—that you have helped a fellow-creature, and relieved his distresses, will be pleasures worth enjoying—an intellectual feast, that cannot be procured in the ball room.

Bring forward your greatest advocate for balls and dances, and he would shudder at the idea of being snatched from the floor of the ballroom, to stand before God in judgement. And incontrovertible proof, that balls are wicked.

Yet, while some people disapproved of dances, many did not. Friedrich Gerstäcker, who traveled through the Arkansas Ozarks from 1838 to 1842, wrote about a rather elaborate dance, given at the expense of a farmer who was running for the legislature, held in 1841:

The sound of a solitary fiddle had been perceptible at a distance, and sure enough, when I arrived, I found dancing going on amongst the younger folks, in one of the wings of the double house. . . . I amused myself with looking on, and watching the arrivals, who thronged in from all ends and corners of the state. A great number of the young women were light and graceful figures, and looked very interesting on horseback, their cheeks flushed with their quick ride. But they seemed as if they were going on a pilgrimage, instead of coming to a ball,—for each fair dame had a bundle of tolerable size in her saddle-bow. . . .

Meantime a long table was laid out before the house, and surrounded with chairs, benches, &c.; but as it was impossible for all to find seats at once, the ladies were accommodated first, and waited upon by the gentlemen. The dinner consisted of roast beef, roast pork, potatoes, sweet potatoes, maize bread, cakes, and coffee and milk, and went off very well. . . . A case of wine for the ladies . . . was soon emptied. After dinner, a speech was made to the assembled public, in honor of the birth-day of the United States, and then dancing commenced again. Picturesque groups were formed here and there, occupied in various ways. In one place, a party of strong-built, sun-burnt figures lounged at full length on the grass, relating their shooting adventures; further on, two figures, astride a fallen tree, were playing a game of cards; in another place, a party leaping with a heavy stone in each hand, to give them more impetus; and a row of big fellows were taking their siesta under the trees . . . Kean [Gerstäcker's companion] and I sauntered about amongst the various groups, and occasionally visited the ball-room—if the interior of a log-house, about sixteen feet by twenty, can be so called. The air within was hot, almost to suffocation, but the sight was at times too pretty, at times too comic to be quickly deserted. Indeed, most of the girls, beating time with their little feet in jigs, reels, and hornpipes, were pretty enough to chain to the spot any worshipper of natural beauty. . . .

Towards evening I joined in a game of cards. Whiskey bottles passed round, and many of the party were right merry. Having had enough of cards . . . I squeezed through the crowd at the door, into one of the corners right opposite to the musician. This functionary was in a rather capricious humor passing abruptly from the wildest allegro to the most dolorous of the dolefuls, and then breaking off suddenly to ask me for a quid of tobacco. On my answering that I had none, he inflicted a couple of rough strokes on his poor instrument, expressing, in coarse language, a most disagreeable wish respecting the eyes of all the company, on account of the dryness of his throat, which had only had the contents of two bottles of whiskey down it, looked wildly round, began to cry, and fell sobbing on the neck of [a] thin man in [a] blue coat . . . He was seized by the arms and legs, and unceremoniously carried out.

Dancing, of course, ceased during this little intermezzo, and one of the party offered to find a sober fiddler; but as the amusement would have been interrupted too long by waiting for him, a tall lad placed himself in front of the chimney, turned up his sleeves with the utmost gravity, bent his knees a little, and began slapping them in time with the palms of his hands; in two minutes all was going on with as much spirit as before.

At length the promised musician arrived, not however in the promised condition; but a connoisseur near me remarked that he would do till twelve o'clock.

To my astonishment, I observed several of the young ladies in white dresses, whom I was almost sure I had seen before in dark dresses; but, as I never paid much attention to such things, I thought I must have been mistaken. An American, however, told me that I was quite right, and that most of them had already changed their dresses three times, and, if I kept a lookout, he continued, I should see that some of them would change again. This, indeed, was the case. Some changed their dresses five times between noon and the following morning. It would be as incorrect to dance for a whole night in the same dress as in Europe to appear without gloves, which latter articles were thought quite unnecessary here. . . .

A little after twelve the old American's prophecy came to pass, and the second fiddler was carried out and laid on the grass, while a third was soon found to take his place (in *Wild Sports in the Far West*, pp. 220-24).

Most square dances consist of a warm-up in which the dancers join hands and circle first to the left and then to the right. Then they perform a left-hand turn (called an "allemande left"), usually with their corner (the person next to them in the square who is not their partner). Next, the man swings the woman and they promenade (the couple dances side by side both facing counterclockwise around the ring with the man on the inside). Then the actual figure is performed and, in many dances, the warm-up is done again to conclude the dance. Among the most popular square dances in the Ozarks are those such as Corner Girl in which all the dancers are moving most of the time. Some dances, such as Wave the Ocean and Sally Gooden, which involve every man dancing with every woman in the square, are quite complicated. Others, such as Indian File, in which the dancers follow the lead in file (supposedly in imitation of an Indian dance), are relatively simple.

Generally the dance tempo is not very fast, usually varying from 100 to 120 beats per minute, but this is not uniform throughout the Ozarks. For many years, dancers in Douglas County, Missouri, have been known to like their dance music much faster than dancers in most other parts of the Ozarks. A tempo of 140 beats per minute would be considered breakneck speed for most square dancers but is just a comfortable tempo for Douglas County dancers. Whatever the tempo, a complete square is rather lengthy, lasting anywhere from fifteen to twenty minutes.

In many communities play-parties were held in lieu of square dances. These were essentially dances without stringed instruments. Instead, the dancers merely sang the music, and the lyrics frequently included instructions for the dance figures. Sometimes, as in Cleburne County, Arkansas, for religious reasons play-parties were the only type of dancing permissible in a community. As Evalena Berry writes: "Dancing in Cleburne County was frowned upon by the churches from the time the congregation at Palestine Baptist Church voted in 1869 against 'dancing and frolican.' But young people continued to have their play-parties where the games were square dancing games such as 'Backstep a Little If You Can't Jump Josie.' At one time in the late 1920's public dances in Heber Springs were forbidden by city ordinance. The dance enthusiasts got around that by sending written invitations and they continued to hold their monthly dances above Haywood's store" (in *Time and the River*).

Sometimes, though, it was merely the lack of instrumentalists that resulted in a play-party; if no fiddler, banjoist, or guitar player was available, any dancelike activity had to be conducted without such instruments. Still, some communities had both play-parties and dances, so it wasn't always a case of one or the other. Play-parties and dances can be thought of as parallel and supplementary forms that fulfilled slightly different functions. The term "play-party" suggests a game or play, not a notion that is included in the word "dance."

Play-parties were also known as "bounce-arounds," "socials," "sociables," and "frolics." This last term was used very broadly to refer to any occasion in which a group of men and women met for social enjoyment. Another less-common name for the play-parties is given by a man who grew up in southeast Kansas: "We referred to them as 'pound parties' because each person or couple would bring a 'pound' of candy, cookies, or fruit."[1]

The play-parties were organized in an informal way:

Usually one or two young men in the neighborhood looking for diversion and entertainment would hit on the idea of a play-party.

They would ride a horse, if they had one, or walk, to one of the most likely neighbors and ask, "How about a party at your house tomorrow night?"

Usually the neighbor was agreeable, as young and old enjoyed play-parties, so off the young fellows went, going from one neighbors' to another inviting every one in the neighborhood.

Many Ozark homes were small, with rough native lumber floors, and more often than not, a bed in the front room which had to be taken down and any other furniture they might have, moved out to make room for the folks to play the party games, which were not much different than square dancing except we danced to singing instead of a fiddle. We didn't mind the rough floors, and in the summertime we sometimes played in the front yard even though some of them were pretty rocky. No one thought of such a thing as serving refreshments, except once in a while a pan of apples was passed to the group.[2]

Madlyn Walters of Jerome, Idaho, who grew up in the Ozarks, recalls three of the most popular play-parties in her childhood community.

These are some of the games we played when I was a kid in the Ozarks:

Skip to My Lou

Skip, skip, skip to my Lou,
Skip, skip, skip to my Lou,

Skip, skip, skip to my Lou,
Skip to my Lou, my darling.

Skip a little faster, skip to my Lou,
etc.

Can't get a red bird a blue bird will do, etc.

I'll get another one prettier than you, etc.

Here Comes Susie

Couples form two lines facing each other. One couple promenades between the couples as this verse is sung:

Here comes Susie, Susie, Susie,
Here comes Susie, Susie, Susie,
Here comes Susie, Susie, Susie,
Susie, Susie my gal.

Then couples part and go to each end of line, couples in line join hands across and form arch, as this verse is sung:

Peeping at Susie, Susie, Susie,
etc.

The boy chases the girl as the group sing:

I'll catch Susie, Susie, Susie,
etc.

The game continues until all couples have performed.

Happy Was the Miller Boy

Couples form circle with odd one in middle. As the song is sung the odd one tries to steal a pardner as the changes are made.

Happy was the miller boy
Lived by the mill.
Mill turned around with a free good will.
One hand on the hopper,
The other on the sack,
The old man bowled out turn right back.

Happy was the miller boy
Lived by the mill.
Mill turned around with free good will.

One hand on the hopper,
The other on the pole,
The old man bowled out do-si-do.[3]

Robert Lee Wolf of Coffeyville, Kansas, recalls two others that were popular in his community during the years from 1935 to 1940:

Go In and Out the Window

Go in and out the window,
Go in and out the window,
Go in and out the window,
For we have gained this day.

(The person chosen to be "it" goes in and out the circle of dancers who make "windows" by holding joined hands high.)

Go forth and choose your lover,
Go forth and choose your lover,
Go forth and choose your lover,
For we have gained this day.

("It" goes inside the circle, and as the dancers sing, he goes to someone of the opposite sex and chooses her or him as his or her "lover.")

I kneel because I love you,
I kneel because I love you,
I kneel because I love you,
For we have gained this day.

(Self explanatory. The shy one would insist—"I kneel because I have to," etc.)

One swing and then I'll leave you,
One swing and then I'll leave you,
One swing and then I'll leave you,
For we have gained this day.

(Couple in center swing as they sing. Others in the circle do likewise.)

One kiss and then I'll leave you,
One kiss and then I'll leave you,
One kiss and then I'll leave you,
For we have gained this day.

(Couple in center kiss. The chosen one remains and the one who was originally "it" returns to the circle and the dance is repeated.)

Shoo Fly

Shoo, fly, don't you bother me;
Shoo, fly, don't you bother me;
Shoo, fly, don't you bother me;
For I belong to somebody.

(Boys go about circle in right-left grand. Girls remain in position.)

I do, I do, I do,
But I cannot tell you who,
I do, I do, I do,
But I cannot tell you who.

(Boy swings the girl he had touched in the right-left grand as the chorus begins. Usually there was a scuffle so the boy could get the girl he wanted.)[4]

World War Two seems to have been a watershed as far as Ozark play-parties were concerned. They had thrived up until that time, although in

1937 Ben Botkin, in his study of play-parties, said that the form had reached its height a generation or two earlier and then began to die out very quickly. The last traditional play-party held in Stone County, Arkansas, took place in 1956 in the community of Pleasant Grove, thirteen miles from Mountain View. By then they were essentially a thing of the past, and after 1956 play-parties became a matter of history, surviving only in museums and books.

There are several explanations as to why play-parties died out. Some agree with Robert Wolf, who explains, "the parties in our area died out as the group of young people of my age scattered as the result of marriage, service, and work."[5] However, every generation had grown up, married, and worked, yet the play-party survived for generations. What seems more likely is that other possibilities for entertainment became available. It is also possible that the function play-parties fulfilled, i.e., a way to play games, disappeared in most rural communities. But those who grew up with this activity have many fond memories. As one man from Willow Springs, Missouri, put it, "they now have more exciting pastimes, but how could they be more pleasurable?"[6]

FOLKSONGS AND BALLADS

The term "folksong" is used both in a general way to refer to all songs in folk tradition and in a more specific manner to distinguish between types of traditional songs. In the latter sense it refers to lyric songs, called folksongs, as opposed to narrative songs, called ballads. In this sense, most play-party songs are properly labeled folksongs. Most folksongs, such as the following example, seem to suggest a story but never quite get around to developing it:

> Black your boots and make them shine,
> Make them shine, make them shine,
> Black your boots and make them shine,
> Shiloh, Shiloh, Shiloh 'Liza Jane.
>
> Oh, the river was up, the water was deep,
> The tide was swift and strong,
> And many a soldier's heart grew weak
> As we went marching on,
> Shiloh, Shiloh, Shiloh 'Liza Jane.[7]

Ballads, on the other hand, do tell a story, as is evident from the following text:

The Creole Girl

It was on one Friday morning
I bid New Orleans adieu.
I made my way to Jackson
Where I was supposed to go.
Mid swamps and alligators
I made my weary way.
It was there I met that Creole girl
On the lake of Pontchartrain.

I said unto that Creole girl,
"My money to me is no good.
If it wasn't for the alligators
I'd sleep out in the woods."
"Oh, welcome, welcome stranger
Although our home is plain
We'll never turn a stranger down
On the lake of Pontchartrain."

She took me to her Mother's house
She treated me quite well.
Her hair in golden ringlets
Hung down [*sic*] her shoulders fell.
I tried to win her beauty
But I found it all in vain
To win the beauty of the Creole girl
On the lake of Pontchartrain.

I asked her if she'd marry me.
She said it could not be.
That you have a lover
And he was far off at sea.
"Oh, yes you have a lover
And true you shall remain
Until he returns to you again
On the lake of Pontchartrain."

I said unto that Creole girl,
"Your face I shall see no more.
I'll never forget the kindness
Or the cottage by the shore.
When the moving sun shall circle
And sparkling drinks I'll drink.
I'll drink success to that Creole girl
On the lake of Pontchartrain."[8]

Most collectors have focused on ballads but have also generally included many folksongs in their collectanea. Folklorists generally break the traditional ballads found in the Ozarks into three classification categories: Child ballads, broadside ballads, and native American ballads. Child ballads are so called because they are among the 305 ballads included by Francis James Child (1825–1896) in his ten-volume work, *The English and Scottish Popular Ballads* (1882–1898). Child, a Harvard professor, combed hundreds of manuscripts and printed sources to produce a collection of what he considered the best of the English and Scottish popular ballads. In the first volume of his magnum opus, he claimed to have gathered "every valuable copy of every known ballad" (p. vii), a statement that now seems naive and even arrogant. Certainly it was premature, for soon after the publication of Child's major work, ballad collecting in America really got underway. His proclamation is more understandable in light of his view of traditional ballad singing. He did make some attempts to unearth examples of the ballads from oral tradition, but he was convinced that, for all practical purposes, folk balladry was extinct. Shortly after the publication of his final volume, folksong collectors began to prove Child wrong by seeking out and recording variants and versions of his 305 songs from folksingers. In many cases these collectors ignored everything else in their search for the gems canonized by Child. This antiquarian attitude was still in evidence as recently as 1956 when noted collector Richard Chase proclaimed that "your ballad is not a true folk ballad unless it is closely kin to one of the 305—no more, no less!—in professor Child's great collection" (in *American Folk Tales and Songs*, p. 229).

It is hardly surprising that the first collectors of Ozark balladry shared the same prejudice that was found among collectors elsewhere in the United States. However, the premier Ozark ballad collector (who was also a collector of many other genres of folklore), Vance Randolph, was aware of the value of including all types of songs found in a singer's repertoire, although he too prized the Child items above all others. His inclusion of songs representative of the total repertoire of folksingers is one of the reasons why his four-volume *Ozark Folksongs* (1946–1950) is justifiably regarded as one of the best American collections.

Among the other ballad categories found in Randolph's work are broadsides. Originally, these were songs printed on one side of a sheet of paper and sold for a small fee. Many of these ballads found in Anglo-American tradition are classified in G. Malcolm Laws's *American Balladry From British Broadsides* (1957). Generally speaking, the songs discussed in Laws are of more recent vintage than Child ballads, which date roughly from 1500 to 1750, while most broadsides treated by Laws date from 1650 to 1900, although there are exceptions in both cases. The lyrics of Child ballads and broadsides are frequently compared to tabloids because they often deal with sensational subjects such as robberies and murders. Of the two ballad texts given below, the first is a Child ballad and the second a broadside. In the first, "Wind and Rain" (a version of Child 10 "The Twa Sisters," a ballad known traditionally by at least twenty-five titles), a man kills his lover because she refuses to marry him. In most versions of the ballad a girl, jealous that a gentleman has courted her younger sister, invites the sister for a walk and drowns her. The form of the story that follows, in which the lover drowns the girl, is not unique to the Ozarks but is more commonly encountered here than elsewhere.

Wind and Rain

Oh, early one morning in the month of May,
Oh, the wind and rain.
Two lovers went fishing on a hot summer's day,
Crying the dreadful wind and rain.

He said to the lady, "Won't you marry me?"
Oh, the wind and rain.
"Then my little wife you'll always be,"
Crying the dreadful wind and rain.

She said, "Oh, no, that will never do."
Oh, the wind and rain.
"I love you but I can't marry you."
Crying the dreadful wind and rain.

He picked up a stick and he knocked her down,
Oh, the wind and rain.
And he threw her in the river to drown,
Crying the dreadful wind and rain.

She floated on down to the mill hill pond,
Oh, the wind and rain,
Where the miller fished her out with his long fishing line,
Crying the dreadful wind and rain.

And he made fiddle pegs of her long finger bones,
Oh, the wind and rain.
And he made fiddle pegs of her long finger bones,
Crying the dreadful wind and rain.

And he made a fiddle bow of her long curly hair,
Oh, the wind and rain.

And he made a fiddle bow of her long curly hair,
Crying the dreadful wind and rain.

And the miller played his fiddle all day,
Oh, the wind and rain.
And the only tune that fiddle would play,
Oh, the dreadful wind and rain.[9]

The second ballad, "The Boston Burglar," was published in 1888, with Michael J. Fitzpatrick credited as author, but it is thought to be of British broadside origin. Certainly predating 1888, it is similar to various ballads about Botany Bay (an especially feared British penal colony in Australia) from which it probably derives. In most American versions, the protagonist is born in Boston rather than London, but in the present text the ballad is localized even more, with the burglar being sent to Little Rock, at one time the site of a state penitentiary.

Boston Burglar

I was born in Boston City, boys,
A city you all know well.
Raised up by honest parents,
The truth to you I'll tell.
Raised up by honest parents,
Raised up most tenderly.
Till I became a sporting young man
At the age of twenty-three.

My character was taken
And I was sent to jail.
Oh, the boys they found it all in vain
To get me out on bail.
The jury found me guilty,
The clerk he wrote it down.
Oh, the judge he passed a sentence, said he,
"You are bound for that Little Rock town."

They put me aboard this east-bound train
One cold December day.
And every station I'd pass through
I could hear those people say,
"There goes that Boston Burglar,
With iron strong chains he's bound down,
For some bad crime or other,
To be sent to that Little Rock town."

There lives a girl in Louisville,
A girl that I love well.
If ever I gain my liberty,
Along with her I'll dwell.
If ever I gain my liberty,
Bad company I will shun.
Likewise nightwalk and gambling,
And also drinking rum.

You who have your liberty;
Please keep it while you can.
And don't run around with boys at night
And break the laws of man.
For if you do you surely will
Find yourself like me,
Just serving out twenty-three long years
In the state penitentiary.[10]

The third type of folk balladry found in the Ozarks is the native American ballad. Most of these date from 1850 to the present, although the oldest such ballad still sung in the Ozarks, "The Rattlesnake Song" (more commonly known as "Springfield Mountain"), is generally thought to date from 1761 when a Timothy Myrick died in Farmington, Connecticut, from a snakebite. (Not everyone agrees that this ballad can be traced back that far. One person who didn't was the late ballad authority Phillips Barry [1880–1937]. For his views see G. Malcolm Laws, *Native American Balladry: A Descriptive Study and a Bibliographical Syllabus*.) Like Child ballads and broadsides, native American ballads deal largely with scandals and tragedies, although themes of American history and development are also found. The most commonly encountered native American ballads in the Ozarks are included in G. Malcolm Laws's *Native American Balladry*, a study and classification system first published in 1950 and revised in 1964. Nevertheless, a number of native American ballads very popular with Ozark folksingers are not found in Laws's book, primarily because they are known to have originated in the popular music industry. Songs such as "The Fatal Wedding," "Little Rosewood Casket," and "Boys in Blue" are omitted on such grounds. Also missing are ballads that are confined to a fairly small area in a region. Thus, songs such as the following ballad about Lee Mills, who was hanged in Cleburne County, Arkansas, in 1898, do not appear in Laws. It has undeniably entered folk tradition, but its popularity is confined to the few counties near where the crime occurred.

Lee Mills

Lee Mills is what I call my name;
Was once without a murder's stain.
You have heard the story told
Of how I came to be so bold.

'Twas on one bright, sunshiny day
When Will Hardin led me astray;
He caused me to commit a crime,
And now I am condemned to die.

Many a night I've lain awake,
Praying to God for pity's sake.
He has pardoned all my sins at last
And has forgive me of my past.

My dear old mother's prayed for me.
Her smiling face I'd love to see;
But death, cold death, has come at last,
And took these troubles from her breast.

Dear rowdy boys, here as I stand,
The sheriff with his rope and my outstretched hands,
You shall hear my experienced words.
Pray don't let one pass you by unheard.

Now here's the scaffold I do see.
It was prepared alone for me;
And I must stand upon it soon,
There to meet my fatal doom.

Now, little girl, we two must part.
To see your tears it breaks my heart.
I would not hate so bad to die,
If it was not leaving you here to weep and cry.[11]

The ballad about Lee Mills is what folklorists refer to as a "good-night" song, because, according to tradition, it was written by a criminal who sang it shortly before his execution. That such attributions are mostly apocryphal has not deterred these legends. Indeed, "goodnight" ballads are quite common among broadsides and native American ballads. There are also many less tragic songs common in traditional Ozark balladry—for example, Child ballads such as "Our Goodman" and "The Farmer's Curst Wife," broadsides such as "Devilish Mary," and the following song, usually called "The Old Woman of Slapsadam" or "The

Wily Auld Carle" in the British Isles but more often in the Ozarks called "Rich Old Lady":

> I knew a rich old lady,
> In London she did dwell.
> She loved her husband dearly,
> But other men twice as well.
> Sing penny a wink she randolph,
> Sing penny a wink she roan.
>
> She went to the doctor
> In hopes that she might find
> Some kind of medicine
> To make her husband blind.
> Sing penny a wink she randolph,
> Sing penny a wink she roan.
>
> She gave him two marrow bones
> And told him to suck them all.
> And then he said, "My dear little wife
> I cannot see you at all."
> Sing penny a wink she randolph,
> Sing penny a wink she roan.
>
> "I think I'm going to drown myself,
> If I only knew the way."
> "Here, let me take you by the hand,
> As you might go astray."
> Sing penny a wink she randolph,
> Sing penny a wink she roan.
>
> Well, she walked on the banks,
> And she walked on the shore.
> And he said, "My dear little wife
> You'll have to push me o'er."
> Sing penny a wink she randolph,
> Sing penny a wink she roan.
>
> She took a few steps backwards
> And run to push him in.
> He just stepped to one side
> And let her tumble in.
> Sing penny a wink she randolph,
> Sing penny a wink she roan.

Now, she began to holler,
And she began to squall.
But he said, "My dear little wife
I cannot see you at all."
Sing penny a wink she randolph,
Sing penny a wink she roan.

The old man being good-natured,
And afeared that she might swim,
He run and cut a big long pole
And pushed her further in.
Sing penny a wink she randolph,
Sing penny a wink she roan.

Now my little song is over
And I won't sing it no more.
But wasn't she a blamed old fool
For not swimming to the shore.[12]

Of the native American ballads currently found in Ozark tradition, several, such as "The Warranty Deed" and "Young Man Who Wouldn't Hoe Corn," are humorous:

Young Man Who Wouldn't Hoe Corn

Come all young ladies and listen to my song
And I'll tell you about a young man that wouldn't raise corn
The reason why I can not tell,
This young man was always well.

In the month of June he planted his corn,
In July he laid it by.
In October there came a frost;
The seed of his corn this young man lost.

Well, he went right down and peeped right in,
The weeds and the grass were up to his chin.
The weeds and the grass they grew so high
They caused this young man for to cry.

Well, he'd go right down to his near neighbor's land,
He'd go there a-courtin' as sure as you're born.
"Kind sir, have you made your corn?"

"Well, yes, my dear" in reply,
"Yes, my dear, I've laid it by.

I've tried and tried and tried in vain;
I don't believe it's going to raise one grain."

"Well, a healthy young man that won't raise corn
Is the laziest that ever was born.
Single I am and single I'll remain.
A lazy man I won't maintain."

Come all young ladies and listen to my song
And I'll tell you about a young man that wouldn't raise corn.
The reason why I can not tell,
This young man was always well.[13]

An Ozark stringband, Corning, Arkansas, 1918. The cello was not a rarity at that time in such organizations. (Photo from the author's collection)

A discussion of Ozark folk music and singing must include some mention of country and bluegrass music, especially since they are often considered synonymous with folk music. Both are commercial forms, but to some extent the equation is justified, because initially country music was derived from folk music. Although many rural performers made recordings as far back as the late nineteenth century, commercial country music is generally thought to have been established in June 1922 when Alexan-

der Campbell "Eck" Robertson, a native of the Ozarks who grew up in Texas, and Henry Gilliland, a seventy-four-year-old fiddler from Altus, Oklahoma, made some unsolicited recordings for the Victor Talking Machine Company. In the following year, 1923, the country music industry had its first recording star, Fiddlin' John Carson. Thereafter, the recordings of rural musicians increased, resulting in a very successful industry that today has moved from folk music to popular music. The change has been gradual. Originally, style, repertoire, and instrumentation were traditional; then the traditional repertoire was replaced by original songs; then instrumentation changed, and now traditional style is all that is left in modern country music. In terms of style, many current country performers owe more to pop music than to folk music.

The first Ozark country musician to make commercial records was Sam Long. Known as Fiddlin' Sam Long of the Ozarks, Long lived in several towns in Kansas and Oklahoma and was noted for winning fiddle contests. It was at one of these, the 1926 Ozark Fiddle Contest in Joplin, Missouri, that he won a recording contract with Gennett Records as part of his prize. Long recorded four sides that did not sell very well. Far more successful were the recordings of James Elton Baker of Zack, Arkansas. As Elton Britt, he became the first Ozark country musician to become a recording star. In 1942 he became world famous as the first country singer to be awarded a gold record, for his recording of "There's a Star Spangled Banner Waving Somewhere." Since that time numerous other Ozark performers have become notable country musicians.

Bluegrass is a type of country music that, in its traditional form, employs the repertoire common in commercial country music from 1925 to 1955, or songs written in that style. Because the genre is named after Bill Monroe's Blue Grass Boys, it is often stated that Monroe invented the music. This is an oversimplification, because bluegrass, like most musical forms, evolved over a period of time and cannot be attributed to a single individual. Defined briefly, bluegrass is a successful blending of elements from various earlier styles, most notably string-band music, usually played by four to seven musicians. Prominent features of bluegrass are "Scruggs-style" banjo, guitar and string bass used mainly as rhythm instruments, high-pitched singing, and extensive use of duple meter. Bluegrass is essentially an exhibition form of music rather than being dance music. Also, bluegrass songs, at least traditional ones, reflect rural rather than urban concerns.

Bluegrass is a relatively modern type of music, dating from the 1940s, and the name has been applied only since the late 1950s. Nevertheless, many people use the term to refer to any acoustic country music suggestive of pre–World War Two styles. This is undoubtedly partly because bluegrass has been included in many folk festivals and because traditional bluegrass consists of songs typical of an older and more folk-related form of country music. However, it is more accurate to think of bluegrass, as well as country, as influences on folk music rather than as folk music forms.

CHAPTER 6

Games and Entertainment

While children, adolescents, and adults all have traditional games, much more is known about the games of Ozark children than about those of the other two groups. Still, some of the earliest collections of Ozark folklore included some information about games played by adults. Frequently, these involved some form of betting and, as the following account by Silas Turnbo indicates, in a few instances games were taken a bit too seriously:

One day Mort Herrean who lived on Shoal Creek and John Tabor who lived on Big Creek went to Dubuque together. Herrean got involved in a row with Jim Cheek over a game of Crack a Blow as it was called. It was played in a house by throwing up a silver quarter and if it stopped directly over a joint in the floor or nearest to it, the one that tossed it up won the game which was for a small sum or a drink of liquor. If there was a tie, it was played over again.

During the day, Mort Herrean and Jim Cheek engaged themselves in this game which was played in Bob Trimble's grocery store. Herrean soon won three drinks of whiskey off of Cheek and he paid his opponent two of the drinks but refused to pay the third one by denying that Herrean won it. The latter kept insisting on Cheek to pay it and the man flatly refused to do so and at last he told Mort Herrean if he demanded it any more, he would cut his throat. This enraged Herrean but he made no reply to the threat of the man Cheek but stepped out and picked up a stone unobserved and concealed it and stood near the grocery store and waited for Cheek to come out, who by this time was very drunk. When the drunken fellow tottered out of the store, he did not see Herrean standing there waiting for his appearance. Just as he got on the outside onto the street and after he had passed Herrean a few feet, the latter hurled the stone against the man and he fell senseless and without uttering a groan.

As soon as Herrean hit Cheek, he and Tabor mounted their horses and started home. After they had forded the river and were riding through the river bottom in the Jake Nave Bend, Tabor said, "Mort, you have killed that man and you may be hung for it." To which Mort replied, "I cannot help it, he ought to have paid me that drink of whiskey that he owed me." Neither one of them did not seem uneasy about Cheek and never knew whether he was dead or alive until one week afterward when Herrean went back to Dubuque to find out. Cheek was not dead but he was not in town, his friends had taken him home. Bob Trimble said that after Herrean and Tabor had left the village and when Cheek had revived from the shock, he said, "Bob, something went wrong with me. Something fell on me or I was kicked by a mule, I don't know which" (in *Turnbo's Tales of the Ozarks* pp. 106–7).

As will be shown later, the game Turnbo called "Crack a Blow" is a drinking game that has survived in several variations to the present day.

Then, as now, horse races were one of the most popular activities involving betting. Today, though, betting involves much higher stakes and is more organized than most nineteenth-century races, one of which is described as follows:

The Bill Adams farm just above where the town of Protem in Taney County, Missouri, now stands was once a noted spot for horse racing on a small scale to be carried on. These races were of a local character and the gathering of citizens to witness the race was not very large and the betting was not very strong. The race tracks were in the creek bottom.

Mort Herrean was among the sportsmen who met there with others occasionally to while away the time of running their horses over the tracks and betting small amounts on the races. One day a few years after Jet Chaffin settled the land where Protem now is, he and Good Madewell ran a horse race here. Each man bet a rifle gun and a few were present to see the race come off. Hiram Bias and Jet Chaffin were selected as judges at the outcome. Good Madewell's wife and Becca Chaffin, wife of Jet Chaffin, were also present and seated themselves near the tracks to watch the horses run through.

As soon as the horses and riders were ready, the race stock was put through under whip and the judges decided that Herrean's horse beat Madewell's twenty-eight feet. This was no encouragement to Madewell's wife and she exclaimed in a loud tone, "I knowed it, I knowed it, I knowed it!" "Yes," said her husband, "I knowed it, too." "Well, you old fool," replied his wife, "what did you run for if you knowed you would lose the race? Now, Good Madewell," continued the disheartened woman, "from now on if you cannot win a race, I want you to quit. You hear my voice, do you." And her husband said he did and the spectators and those interested took their departure to their respective homes (in *Turnbo's Tales of the Ozarks*, pp. 112–13).

These days, of course, horse races are carried out in much more grandiose facilities.

Not all adult games practiced in the nineteenth century involved betting, and neither were they all of an informal nature. In northern Arkansas, organized tournaments of knights flourished in the years immediately following the Civil War. In teams of knights, men took part in contests of tilting or jousting, the purpose being to win the tournament for their home town. Instead of being hurled at humans, the lances were launched at rings suspended by wires, a fairly difficult target to hit from horseback. Exciting and interesting though this version of knighthood must have been, it was nothing but a colorful memory by 1900.

Other games that adults engaged in seem unnecessarily cruel to modern audiences and even to some who participated in them. In *Turn South for Arkansas* by Margie I. Mills, George Washington Dalton describes a popular sporting activity practiced in his younger days, gander pulling:

They were about the cruelest things that you can imagine. I believe that they went out along with dueling. We usually had about one or two a year. Christmas was a favorite time to have them. One that I remember was held at a grist mill. All the men and boys in the surrounding territory would take a turn of corn to mill on Saturday, whether they needed any grinding done or not, as an excuse to go. Two poles were set up about nine or ten feet high and about six or eight feet apart. A beam was set upon the top of the uprights. A gander would be picked clean and have his head greased. The meaner and older the bird the tougher he was and the better the sport. The sportsmen would pay a quarter to pull. This is how it operated. The gander was tied by the feet to the pole with his head hanging down. The contestants got on a mule or a horse and ran the mount under the pole and the gander. The man was allowed to run under the pole three times and grab at the gander's head. The gander went to the man who could pull off the bird's head without being unseated on the bareback mule. When the bird was fresh he would dodge and bob his head until, if a fellow caught it at all, the grease would cause it to slip through his hands. Sometimes a man might swing his weight with an especially tough neck. As soon as the poor old gander wearied down he was less active and an easier victim. It was a great sport but very cruel. I was personally glad when we stopped having them (p. 94).

While adolescents had no games or activities comparable to gander pulling, they did have some very mischievous "games" that some, especially those on the receiving end of the "sport," considered cruel. One such activity was ticktacking, described by a Mount Vernon, Missouri, woman in a book by Grace Hunt Smith:

One summer evening my brothers and two neighbor boys decided it would be fun to go "ticktacking." They fixed the apparatus consisting of a tin can and a long string well treated with resin so when you pulled the string it would make a weird, squeaky sound that could easily wake anyone from a sound sleep. My sisters went with them and I didn't want to be left out so I tagged along.

It was a moonlit night. After the noise started, John Dunn came out on the front porch in his underwear and put his foot upon the banister and looked in each direction. He hollered, "Now, you all had better get away from here and leave me alone." We were crouching low on the ground, so he couldn't see us. Mr. Dunn went back inside the house and soon the boys started up the screeching again. Here Mr. Dunn came with a shotgun and fired up into the air. And, that did it!

When he went inside, we all ran home and we were so scared we didn't talk about it, but that ended the "ticktacking" forever at that house (in *Buttermilk and Cracklin' Bread*, pp. 51–52).

Ticktacking is still occasionally practiced, but today's adolescents generally have other ways of getting into mischief.

Of course, not all games and activities were of a cruel or mischievous nature. Many entertainments were basically excuses to bring members of the opposite sex together for innocent fun. One such was a "candy breakin'," an entertainment that had disappeared by World War Two. In her article "Candy Breaking: Country Social," Helene Stallcup describes a typical candy breakin':

Basically "candy-breaking" constituted nothing more than the breaking of small pieces of candy into *smaller* pieces. Only the manner in which this was accomplished made it entertaining.

First, the household head would have to make one of his twice-yearly trips into town. Among the needed supplies he brought back would be a dozen or so sticks of hard candy; or more, according to the number of expected guests. These would be stored safely away until the neighbors could be summoned for a social.

At a convenient time, word went out over the hills that the Yandells, Ellisons, Moores; or some neighbor was having a "candy-breaking" next Saturday night. If school was in session the message circulated rather quickly. The postmaster could also be counted on to spread the news. Travelers on horseback would be sure to mention a Saturday night "candy-breaking" before they left. Socials ranked high in news order, along with a "burnout," and Zeke Taylor's plow-horse getting foundered.

On the night prescribed, every hill and hollow in the school district would have shed its occupants for the party. Even so, the gathering might not number more than three dozen people, for there were more hills than occupants in those days.

Though a "candy-breaking," by its name, might seem directed toward the younger group, it was never limited to children, or even to young people. Everyone in the family came along, including an occasional cautious hound who managed to trail his owners through the woods.

In preparation for the party, beds were taken down and removed from the living room. Extra chairs, stools, and trunks were brought in and placed against the walls. As a final stretching measure, the boys brought in a couple of long boards, and laid them across two chairs. Grandma placed folded quilts over these boards. They became very satisfactory benches unless a boy got too rowdy, and spilled a group of young ladies on the floor. There were times, then as now, when boys chose unfortunate ways of getting attention.

Groups began arriving before dark, carrying lanterns for the return trip late in the evening. Those from farther away came in wagons. The young bucks usually came on horseback, galloping up in a dash—making a daring display of horsemanship. For effect, it was much more satisfying than the screech of brakes, and spinning of wheels displayed by their modern counterparts.

When the party began, young folks seated themselves around the living room wall, and the older folks took a chair in the kitchen. The host would usually have the candy in a shoe box, take it out, and break it into as many pieces as possible. The shorter the pieces, the more interesting the action thereafter.

The game would begin at some point in the circle, usually with one of the younger children. Youngsters usually chose the longest pieces, and "broke" with friends of the same sex. Friendly wrestling ensued among the boys as each tried to get the most candy. Hands and heads bumped together after stray chunks. While older children enjoyed the competition, smaller children received their pieces without breaking.

But the fun began when the bold young men got a turn. With a certain young lady in mind, the young man chose the shortest possible chunk of candy, and the young lady for his partner. The candy was, of course, too short to be broken with their fingers, and would have to be divided in the next prescribed manner. They would have to *bite* it in two. In a very strict moral society this was a tantalizing bit of permissiveness, and brought on a good deal of horseplay and lively reactions.

Unfortunately, back then the prettiest girls and the handsomest boys got chosen first, too, but everyone had a turn, and it was considered a breech of etiquette to refuse to "break" with anyone.

A generous fire in the fireplace, with popcorn frequently passed around, combined with the candy to create a procession to the waterbucket. The young men, especially, developed an intensive thirst, for as the water dwindled a couple was chosen to go to the spring for more. Since it was quite dark on the way to the spring, this was a very desirable chore. However, little courting was accomplished on these trips for several youngsters were loosed out the back door, by watchful mamas, to scare the couple along.

Often the breaking culminated in a songfest of hymns and old hill melodies. At a fairly late hour small children, sound asleep, were slung over their papas' shoulders for the trip home. Young men offered the ladies rides home on the backs of their horses. Lanterns and cheery voices faded into the dark hills (in *The Ozarks Mountaineer* December 1976, p. 24).

Any social activity involving both sexes had the potential to initiate romances, and candy breakin's were no exception. George Dalton's little trick described here probably was repeated by numerous swains: "Each boy paid his dime and chose a partner with whom he wished to break candy. The short sticks of peppermint candy were used. The more daring couples bit the pieces. There was one regulation that the biting must go on in the presence of the entire company in the middle of the floor. George dared Adeline to bite with him. She accepted and they took the middle of the floor. Addy reached up to bite and George sucked in the short piece of candy, kissing her square on the lips. 'That war the sweetest kiss I ever stole.' He chuckled while Addy flushed pink after seventy years" (in *Turn South For Arkansas*, p. 95).

Those families that didn't condone dancing did allow play-parties and a number of party games. Some of these were ancient and widely known—hull gull was an American version of a game that dates back to the fourth century B.C.—while others were more modern. Among the more recent were such games as hurly burly, blow the coal, and poor pussy. In hurly burly, one person tells each player what to do to a certain person, while another tells each player whom to do it to. After everyone has been instructed, players say "hurly burly," and the players dash to their victims, to do as they have been told. Frequently players trying to reach their victims discover that they are someone else's victim. In blow the coal, the object is to suspend a needle or pin from the ceiling and stick it into a live coal, around which a circle of players, each one blowing with all his might, has gathered. The strongest blowers blow the coal at weaker blowers, with the result frequently being that the coal is blown into a player's mouth or face. In the game poor pussy, one player who is "it" imitates a cat and tries to provoke laughter from the other players. When he or she succeeds, then the player who laughed becomes "it."

Among other folk games practiced by Ozark adults are mumble peg, a marbles game called hoss in, and washers. Washers is a pitching game that takes its name from the object pitched—a small metal washer. This is thrown from varying distances, usually about fifteen feet, at one or more holes in the ground. As few as two or as many as eight players are involved, and it seems to be popular with all age groups. Generally, it is purely recreational, but occasionally betting is involved. Like most of the other games mentioned here, mumble peg, hoss in, and washers are not unique to the Ozarks; all three are well known throughout the South.

Popular with young adults, particularly those in college, are various drinking games. The main purpose of most of these games is to get people drunk, but their secondary purpose is to provide amusement and a socializing opportunity for everyone involved. Many of these games involve simple physical actions, while several, such as pat, which is described by a student at the University of Arkansas, make use of cards:

The object of the game is that you have a deck of cards. And each player gets five cards. Deuces are wild. You can make them anything you want to. When you get two of a kind you have to lay them down. And, when you get down to one card in your hand, you have to say "pat." If you don't say "pat," it's a violation or you have to take a shot of whiskey out of a shot glass. But, when you discard, like if the person on your left is next, and somebody else around the table gets to it before that person does, it goes to them and then its their turn. You can skip people all the way through the game. . . . And, when you lay down like two tens and you have a two that's wild and you have a five and you lay it down and you have one more card, you have to discard. You discard and you win and the person with the highest hand has to take it, has to take a shot of whiskey.[1]

As in virtually all of the drinking games, the fun for contestants in pat is to see who can get drunk fastest.

Some drinking games, such as quarters, the modern version of the game Turnbo called "crack a blow," involve money, but not in a betting sense:

You take not a tall glass but a medium-sized glass where you can bounce a quarter into it. And you get on a solid wood table or a table that has got some bounce to it. You take a quarter and you bounce it. If it goes in the cup, you point at somebody who you want to drink. Then they drink it. And it's kinda like pat, if you make three in a row then you get to make a rule. Like if you make six in a row, you know, then you got two different rules. And you write the rules down. And the object is, basically to see who can get fucked up the most.[2]

Other drinking games, such as bizz buzz, involve no equipment but consist of a complicated routine involving numbers:

As many people as you want, they sit in a circle, you need at least four people. Okay, and the way that you play the game is . . . you start going clockwise, and the first person will say one, two, three, four. Five will be bizz. Any multiple of five or any number ending in five, the person will say "bizz" instead of the number. Now, if you're going clockwise, as soon as he says "bizz," it changes directions. Bizz is a multiple of five and you change direction. Buzz is multiple of seven or anything ending in seven you change direction. And you just keep going around and around and changing directions and a person who misses the buzz, or the bizz has to take a drink.[3]

Some games, such as one called spoons, are nondrinking games that are adapted to become drinking games:

The objective of spoons is to get trashed, as usual, you can play it with beer or mixed drinks. Now the way the game is played, say as an example we have five people around the table, we need four spoons. One less spoon than the amount of players playing the game. Okay, the way you play it, first of all you get a deck of cards. Take out the two jokers. The objective is to get four of a kind. Now, say one person has the cards, we'll go in a clockwise direction. The first person who has the cards just picks up a card. Wait a second. Wait a second. All right, you give everyone around the circle, five people playing, give them each four cards.

Okay, now the person who's dealing when we start the game, says "go," he picks up a card. If he doesn't need the card or want the card, puts it down, the next person takes it. Okay, the next person if he needs it takes it, or if not he puts it down. The cards just keep going around in a circle and the first person just keeps picking up a card. Now the first person with four of a kind picks up a spoon. Now anyone who sees a person pick up a spoon needs to pick up a spoon right away. The last person who doesn't pick up a spoon loses the game and drinks whatever beverage they're serving.[4]

These drinking games, and others, are sometimes played by non-college-age people at private parties, but in most cases it is college-age Ozarkers who participate in these activities. As they grow older they tend to abandon such games.

Much more is known about the games played by Ozark children than about those involving other age groups. There are many reasons for this situation, but two are especially noteworthy. One is that the earliest students of games, such as William Wells Newell, focused on children's games, and collectors of folklore tend to follow the lead of their predecessors. The other is that many game collections are the result of adults giving an interviewer examples of memory culture, and in these situations informants generally try to recall the earliest games they can remember playing. Many collections, focusing on an era fifty years and more in the past when there were lots of one- and two-room schools throughout the Ozarks, emphasize the games children played at recesses in these small schools. Several of these games, such as leapfrog and rounders, a variation on baseball, are still played, but there are many others that are now rare or are no longer played at all. The tag games of blackman and darebase, described below, are among those played in the past. The following versions of these, as well as of hatball and sowhole, are taken from Gilbert C. Kettelkamp's "Country-School Games of the Past":

Blackman

The game required two bases at each end extending the width of the playing field. The bases were usually scratches on the ground or grass, or lines made by sticks or boards placed end to end. Fences at sides of the school ground or the school building itself could serve as boundary lines.

Before the game began it was necessary to select one or more persons to be "it." The players had various ways for making such choices. Players might race from one base to the other; the last one there would be "it." If this happened to be a small pupil, he would usually be given the privilege of selecting a helper. For this he would usually select someone who was agile and fast. Other factors often also helped to determine the last to reach the base line. Pupils would gang up on a certain player with the intention of causing him to arrive last at the base line.

BASE LINE

BASE LINE

Layout for Blackman

They might intentionally bump into him to cause him to stumble or fall down so that he would be left behind. But the victim might also have a trick in mind; he might just as easily trip up one of the plotters and leave the latter sprawling on the ground while he laughed and raced on to the base line. No one regarded such tricks as unethical. They were just a part of the preparation for the game. A pupil seldom showed any great displeasure at being "it."

The "it" players roamed between the bases while the others tried to run between the bases without being tagged. They were safe only while on one of the bases. If they were tagged, they became a member of the "it" group. The game continued until all had been tagged or, as most often happened, the school bell rang to end play.

Darebase

The layout for darebase was similar to that for blackman, but the action of the latter was considerably more involved. The change in layout required that about eight feet in front of each base line, and running parallel to it, there had to be a darebase line. That line could also be laid out by extending a scratch on the ground or by placing sticks end to end.

To start the game two teams were needed who spread out over the length of their home-base line. Then one or more players from one team moved downfield with the intention of touching the opponents' darebase line. It would be to their credit to be able to touch that base and to return to their home base without being tagged by an opposing player. It was at that point, however, that the game became complicated. The major objective on the field was for a player to tag an opponent who had left his home base previous to the time the tagger had left his. Hence with groups of players from both teams being active on the field at the same time, confusion was common. Although the last individual to leave his base had the tag on an opponent who had left earlier, he himself was subject to being tagged by a member of the opposite team who had left base after he had. A player legitimately tagged by a member of the opposite team immediately had to return to his captor's base and operate from there as a member of that team. In this way membership of the two teams changed continually.

The ultimate objective, of course, was for one team to capture all of the players, but this seldom happened. The complex nature of the game usually kept both sides fairly well balanced. One aspect of the game that made it even more complicated resulted from the fact that a player could operate out from his opponent's case as well as from his own, that is, providing he could get onto and off of it without being tagged out in the open.

Since the time one left base was such an important aspect of the game, there were continual arguments between players about who had tag on the other. In spite of such arguments the game was highly popular and generally enjoyed by both large and small players. Even a small, lower-grade youngster was at times

```
┌─────────────────────┐
│ HOMEBASE LINE       │
│ DAREBASE LINE       │
│ – – – – – – – – – – │
│                     │
│                     │
│                     │
│                     │
│                     │
│ – – – – – – – – – – │
│ DAREBASE LINE       │
│ HOMEBASE LINE       │
└─────────────────────┘
```

Layout for Darebase

able to tag a large boy or girl who had ventured a bit too close to the home base of his opponents.

Hatball was a game involving throwing a soft ball:

To begin this game players simply placed their hats or caps compactly together on the ground or grass with the bottom sides up. This made it possible for the "it" player to reach far enough to drop the soft ball used into one of the hats. The "it" player then took the ball and moved his arm in a circle over the upturned hat or caps. That motion was to confuse the owners as to where he would drop the ball.

However before he made this move, each of the other players tried to take positions as near to their own headgear as possible. After numerous feints the "it" player dropped the ball into one of upturned items. At the drop every player, except the owner of the cap or hat which had received the ball, dashed away as soon as possible. The owner, meanwhile, seized the ball and from his position tried to hit one of the players running away. If he threw and missed he was out of the game and had to pick up his hat or cap and step aside. Although he was out of the game, he became the "it" man who could next drop the ball.

However if the thrower hit a player after picking up the ball from his hat, the hit player had to run to the point where the ball had rolled and from there try to hit someone else with it. Thus, the action continued until a thrower failed to hit another player. Whenever that happened the one who had missed had to drop out of the game and become the next "it" man. At no time could a player run with the ball; he must throw from the spot where he had retrieved it. If time permitted the game continued until only a single player remained. Naturally he was the winner.

Another interesting ball game was sowhole, a game involving a wooden stick or club:

The players dug a hole in the ground about four inches deep and six inches in diameter; that was the sowhole or goal. Next, the players formed a circle around this goal, and each player except one dug a small hole about two inches deep in front of himself; those holes were the home bases. Of course if the game had been played before, the layout was already available for use as soon as the players took their positions. The circle could be of any size, but one with a radius of from three to five feet was generally most desirable. The home-base holes were spaced somewhat evenly on the circumference of the circle, usually about two to three feet apart. The tag base was, of course, some distance away.

The "it" player or driver tossed the ball into the circle to start the game, and it was his objective to guide it into the sowhole with his club. The other players, however, stationed with the ends of their clubs in their individual holes, were ready to drive the ball away. But when one of them removed the end of the club from his hole, the driver or any other player was free to acquire possession of it

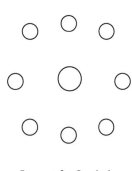

Layout for Sowhole

by placing the end of his club into the hole while the owner was otherwise engaged. Such action naturally resulted in frequent scrambles for possession of holes. Eventually the player who ended up without a homebase hole had to become the new driver. This may or may not have been the individual who just previous to the action had been the driver.

A player on the opposite side of the circle from where the driver happened to be working with his club usually took the risk of driving the ball out or away from the sowhole area. At no time during the action could a player touch the ball with his hands. Every experienced driver knew that the best way for him to control the ball was to herd or coax it along slowly in the hook of his club, that is if it had a hook; in that way he could protect it better from attackers. If he was successful in placing it in the sowhole, all players had to run and touch the tag base with their clubs, then run back to gain possession of a home-base hole again. The player who at the end of the race was left without such a hole had to become the new driver.

It might appear that there was little to gain for a player, other than the driver, to steal a hole from another player. However holes on the side of the circle nearest the tag base were naturally favored because they gave the occupant the advantage of several feet in the race to and from that location. Also, throughout the game there was always the challenge for the less skillful or young player to steal the hole of a good player in order to watch the latter maneuver himself out of his predicament. The former seldom took too much of a chance himself; he usually acquired the hole while the more skillful one was engaged in a skirmish to drive the ball away from the circle of protected holes (in *Mid-America Folklore*, fall 1981, pp. 116–20).

There were many other variations on baseball, such as long-town and town ball, but most of these seem to have disappeared along with the small schools that helped keep them alive. Although informal play has not disappeared, there is much more organized play today than there was in the past and less opportunity to play many of the traditional games that once flourished.

Of the numerous tag games played by children, one that was particularly popular in the late nineteenth and early twentieth centuries was called chickame, chickame, craney-crow. Some idea of the variation in its play is apparent in the following three accounts, the first two from Missouri and the third from Arkansas:

There are three bases: the old witch's base and two home bases for the players. The old witch takes her place at her base and the players all assemble at one of the home bases.

Then all the players chant in unison:

Chickame, chickame, craney-crow

Went to the well to wash his toe,

When he got back the black-eyed chicken was dead.

Then all the players shout, "What time is it, old witch?"

Old Witch: "Time for you to go home."

Players: "Can I get there by candlelight?"

Old Witch: "Yes, if your legs are long and light."

The players all shout, "Watch out that the old witch don't get you!" and start running for the other base. The old witch runs from her base and attempts to tag one or more of the players. All tagged players go and stand at the old witch's base.

Then the procedure is repeated. This continues till all the players are tagged. Then another player is the old witch. The witch's base is movable, depending on the speed of the old witch. A fast runner moves the base further away; a small child as the old witch moves her base closer.

The children formed a line, behind the leader, with hands clasped around the waist of the child in front, much like in a snake-dance, and marched past another player who was called the old lady. Our chant was somewhat different from the one given [by the informant above] but I don't remember the exact wording.

The leader, at the head of the line, would say the chant, asking the old lady what the time was. The old lady would answer any time period that suited her, like "one o'clock," or "two o'clock," in which case the line of children would continue to march on past and then come around past the old lady again; each time they passed, the leader would say the chant and receive an answer. At some time (supposed to be a surprise) the old lady would say, 'Time to eat one of your children', and then she would try to catch one of them. The leader would spread out her arms to keep the old lady from getting past her, and the 'children' or 'chickens' as we called them tried to stay behind the leader, but always had to hold on to the child in front of them. When the old lady caught one of the children, this child would line up behind the old lady in the same manner in which they had been behind the leader. This went on until the old lady had all of the children behind her, whereupon she became the 'leader' and the former leader became the 'old lady.' The children who were caught by the old lady had to follow her when she was trying to catch the others, and when she caught one in the center of the other line, that one dropped out, going behind her to the end of the line. The other line tried to close the gap.

Chickame, chickame, craney-crow;

Went to the well to wash my toe;

When I got back one chicken was gone.

What time is it, old witch?

One child is chosen for the witch. The other children choose one hour, from 1:00 to 12:00, and form in line with hands on shoulders of the child in front.

Marching around, they sing above lines. If the witch answers with the hour chosen, they break line and run to escape being touched or caught. If the witch

names the wrong hour, the line continues the same again and again until the
number is guessed by the witch, or they tire of the game. The one caught by the
witch takes the place of the witch.[5]

RHYMES AND RIDDLES

Very small children were, and still are, frequently read Mother Goose
rhymes, such as:

> Georgie Porgie, pudding and pie,
> Kissed the girls and made them cry.
> When the boys came out to play,
> Georgie Porgie ran away.[6]

Other literary-sounding rhymes, such as the following two, are often
heard:

> Curly locks! Curly locks!
> Wilt thou be mine?
> Thou shalt not wash dishes
> Nor yet feed the swine;
> But sit on a cushion
> And sew a fine seam
> And feast on strawberries, sugar and cream.[7]

> Ladybird, ladybird, fly away home,
> Your house is on fire,
> Your children are gone.
> All but one, and her name is Ann,
> And she crept under the pudding pan.[8]

Other well-known rhymes, however, are clearly not derived from
printed sources. One that was once popular with small children is the
following ditty about Jackie Mariah:

> Jackie Mariah
> Jumped in the fire;
> The fire was so hot
> He jumped in the pot;
> The pot was so black
> He jumped in the crack;
> The crack was so high
> He jumped in the sky;
> The sky was so blue
> He jumped in the flue;
> The flue was so narrow

He jumped in the tallow;
The tallow was so soft
He jumped in the loft;
The loft was so rotten
He jumped in the cotton;
The cotton was so light
He stayed all night.[9]

Most of the rhymes recited by small children were shorter than the Jackie Mariah lines. The humor that is exhibited often seems funnier to the children than to most adults. An example is the following:

Three little monkeys jumping on the bed,
One fell off and broke his head,
He went to the doctor and died anyway.[10]

Some other rhymes are not recited by children but by adults who tell them to children. The following three rhymes are of this type:

Little wind, blow on the hilltop.
Little wind, blow on the plain.
Little wind, blow up the sunshine.
Little wind, blow off the rain.

Hippity hop to the barber shop,
To buy a stick of candy,
One for you and one for me,
And one for sister Annie.[11]

Look! Look!
Where? Where?
Under the chair.
Run! Run!
Now it's done.[12]

Autograph albums are still quite popular with children of the ninth grade and younger. This is a modern continuation of a tradition that started among European university students in the Middle Ages. Beginning in the 1820s, autograph albums became a rage in the United States for about thirty years with people of all ages. After 1850 the custom was perpetuated primarily by school children. Verses written in such albums from 1820 to 1850 were often quite morbid and long; frequently they were taken from "album writers," published books containing material suitable for inscriptions. After 1850 the verses inclined towards humor and were more often from folk tradition than from "writers." Autograph album rhymes used in the Ozarks today may be either humorous or serious, although even the nonhumorous items are not as morbid as the inscriptions commonly used from 1820 to 1850. The following two items are typical of those with somber overtones:

> When I am in some far and distant land,
> Turn to this and read my name.
> Think of a friend so kind and true,
> Who never more will meet with you.[13]

> Roses are red,
> Violets are blue,
> Sugar is sweet,
> So are you.[14]

Many of the humorous album rhymes deal with intimations of marriage, presumably for the purpose of embarrassing the album's owner:

> I love you a lot.
> I love you a plenty.
> I hope we marry before you're twenty.

> The road is wide and full of ditches
> And someday I hope I can patch your britches.

> I love cornbread I do I do.
> And someday I hope I can sleep with you.[15]

Often the humor is in a fake-bawdy vein, changing what would be considered a vulgar last line into something innocuous:

> I went to the creek to take a swim,
> I pulled off my clothes and threw 'em on a limb,
> I pulled off my shoes and threw 'em in the grass,
> I jumped in the water up to my knees.
> The reason this doesn't rhyme is because the water
> wasn't deep enough.[16]

Jumping rope is one of the major activities that involves the use of rhymes. In the nineteenth century, rope jumping was almost exclusively practiced by young boys, but in the twentieth century it is engaged in primarily by young girls. Some of the rhymes used today in the Ozarks, such as the three given below, are heard just about everywhere the tradition of jumping rope exists. The first example is one of the oldest and most widely reported jump-rope rhymes still used in America. The second is one of the most widely traveled of such rhymes. Unlike the first two, the third rhyme doesn't involve counting jumps until one misses but merely sends the jumper out after the rhyme is concluded.

Down in the valley
Where the green grass grows
There sat Melody
As sweet as a rose.
Then came Randy
And kissed her on the cheek.
How many kisses did she get?
One, two, three, . . .[17]

Cinderella dressed in yellow,
Went upstairs to see her fellow,
Made a mistake and kissed a snake,
How many doctors did it take,
1, 2, 3, 4, 5, 6, . . .[18]

I drink coffee, I drink tea.
Send her in with me.
I drink coffee, I drink tea.
Send her out.[19]

As with other folk rhymes used by children, humor is frequently the intent of jump-rope rhymes:

I had an old mule, his name was Jack,
I rode his tail to save his back.
His tail got loose and I fell back,
Whoa Jack.
I put him in the stable,
He crawled through a crack,
And skinned his navel.[20]

Way down south where bananas grow
A grasshopper stepped on an elephant's toe
The elephant said with tears in his eyes
"Pick on someone your own size!"[21]

Riddling is an activity that was once very popular with all age groups, serving as a form of homemade entertainment. Now it is almost exclusively practiced by younger children or by adults trying to entertain smaller children. Many of today's most popular riddles involve a description of animals or insects:

As I went over the hill
There I met my brother Bill.
With a hammer and a nail.
With a cat with nine tails

Through the rock, through the reel,
And the old spinning wheel.
Sheep, shank, shin and bones
Such a riddle was never known.
Answer: maggots or creepers.

As I went over a heap of steeples
There I met a heap of people.
Some was nicker, some was nacker,
Some as brown as tobacco.
Answer: bees.[22]

Others use a confusing, circuitous manner to describe fruit or the plants that bear fruit:

White as snow but snow it's not,
Green as grass but grass it's not,
Red as blood but blood it's not,
Black as ink but ink it's not.

Answer: A blackberry.

Crooked as a rainbow
Teeth like a cat
Guess a lifetime and can't guess that.

Answer: Blackberry briar.[23]

Some riddles refer to implements that were once common in the home:

North, south, east, and west
A thousand teeth in its mouth.

Answer: wool carder.[24]

Others make use of puns:

Railroad crossing without any cars,
Can you spell that without any rs?

Answer: T-H-A-T

As I walked across London Bridge I met a man.
He tipped his hat and drew his cane.
In this riddle I told you his name.

Answer: Andrew.[25]

As I went across London Bridge,
I met a man. If I told his name,
I would be to blame. I told his name five times.

Answer: A man named I.[26]

LITERARIES

A popular form of entertainment for many Ozarkers before World War One was the "literary." Held on Friday nights, the literaries were an eclectic mixture of events ranging from debates to kangaroo courts to spelling bees to ciphering matches, and other programs as well, all designed purely for the entertainment of the audience. Debates were a highlight of most literaries, sometimes constituting the whole program. Topics generally involved historical, philosophical, ethical, or moral questions or focused on issues of international, national, or local importance. A debate could be serious, such as a discussion of whether or not whiskey destroys more lives than war, or frivolous, such as the question of whether or not woman is more attracting to the eye of man than monkeys. The only requirement was that the debate be entertaining to everyone in attendance.

The debating teams usually consisted of adults, although school children were occasionally allowed. Sometimes debate leaders, having chosen their fellow team members, made the principal speeches themselves and allowed the others to speak whenever they thought of a point to make. Debating styles, of course, varied widely, but many people undoubtedly followed the advice given by one of Vance Randolph's informants:

The main thing in debatin' is to get a chanct to speak first and then jump in and mention ever' pint on the other side sayin' how them is pretty good arguments but ever last one of 'em has got a hole in it somewhar and when t'other side gets up they cain't do nothin' only kinder foller long after what you done said cause there ain't nothin' new fer them to fetch out and the jedges mostly thinks well probable he wouldn't ever never figgered out all them things if your side hadn't said 'em first and peers like he ain't makin' no great go out of it no how (in *Ozark Mountain Folks* p. 27).

In some sections of the Ozarks, kangaroo courts rivaled debates as a popular feature of literary programs. The manner in which they were conducted is described in the following remarks from the Ash Grove (Missouri) *Commonwealth*, February 7, 1889:

Lawrenceburg has a moot tribunal of justice known by the uphonious of "Kangaroo Court." It takes cognizance of all manner of real or imaginary offenses "against the peace and dignity of the town." The witnesses are sworn not to tell the truth or anything resembling it. It is a remarkable fact that the poor culprit whose case comes up before this bar has never been known to escape conviction (*Ozark Baptizings*, p. 38).

The laws "violated" were frequently imaginary, and, to add to the hilarity of the event, the indictments were often improbable but usually based upon fact or actual conduct of a defendant, even though the charges were often the exact opposite of a person's real behavior. For example, a well-known teetotaler might be charged with public drunkenness. Paying too much attention to girls, sleeping during church, courting during a literary, refusing to marry, and stealing hogs are typical examples of the offenses with which those brought before the kangaroo court were charged. The court consisted of a pickup judge and jury and any other officers of the court that were considered necessary. The role of attorney, either prosecuting or defense, was the most important and was usually reserved for the best talkers in the community. Defendants were almost always found guilty and punished with a fine, usually a nickel to a dollar, that was used to pay for school necessities.

Spelling bees, found at most literaries, were especially popular. Generally the teacher selected the best spellers who then chose others to be on their teams. Contestants could be school children or adults and, of course, the object was to "spell down" the other side. Those who failed to spell the word they had been given correctly sat down, and the word was passed to the other side. The bee began with relatively easy words and continued with progressively more difficult ones until all contestants but the champion were eliminated. Sometimes the joy of winning was the champion's only reward, but often a book, quilt, or some similar prize was given.

A correspondent for the Ash Grove, Missouri, newspaper described a typical spelling bee held in that town in 1897:

The old fashioned spelling match in Chandler's Hall last Friday evening was well attended. After a song, "Old Folks at Home," Ote Weir and Ed Barbee were put up for class leaders. They chose sides until the audience was thinned out. Mrs. Lula Silver gave out the words from an old blue backed speller. Clint Nicholson on Ote's side was the first on Ed's side to demand a division of the honors of the evening with Nicholson. Chandler insists he was in dead earnest but the crowd still believes he went down for the fun of it. . . . It was finally narrowed down to Mrs. Doyle and Henry Swindler. Directly Henry went down on "lethargy" and Mrs. Doyle was declared the winner. . . . After a song by Ed Barbee and some light refreshments the meeting was adjourned (in *Ozark Baptizings*, p. 43).

Ciphering matches were less popular than spelling bees for at least two reasons. One was that the ability to figure, while prized as a part of necessary education, was not believed to represent "learning" as much as the ability to spell. The other was that the command to divide, add, or multiply several figures did not have the dramatic appeal of a spelling contest. Ciphering matches were most popular when the competition was between two schools. Frequently the star cipherer of the host school was pitted against a star cipherer selected by the visitors. The winner of the first problem competed against a second challenger and ciphered as long as he or she could stand. Both speed and form were necessary, as cipherers had to arrive at the correct answer first and also show all of their computations in correct arrangement.

Closing-of-School Programs

One activity that disappeared along with one- and two-room schools was the closing-of-school programs. These took place on the last day of school and were divided into two parts, with the first consisting of a demonstration of the students' abilities in several school subjects and the second being a literary-type entertainment. Parents and residents of the school district attended such programs, and at some point during the day the teacher set aside some time for remarks by these patrons. As Guy Howard remarked, "It would have been a grave error to have omitted this closing day courtesy to the patrons. In the hill country one must be very sure that he has a substitute that will meet with ready approval before he deviates in the slightest way from the usual way of doing things" (in *Walkin' Preacher of the Ozarks*, p. 165).

Typically, the closing-of-school programs were rather lengthy. Even so, the eighty-five items scheduled for presentation at the Phelps, Missouri, school in 1893 was unusual (in *Ozark Baptizings*, p. 58). No matter how many presentations were slated, the final act before dismissal was distribution of candy to all the children in the audience by the teacher. After that, everyone usually went home happy.

Folk Narratives

The term "folktale," like folk song, is used in two ways: to refer to all folk narratives and specifically to distinguish a type of folk narrative from myths and legends. Myths are traditional narratives believed to be true that are set in the prehistoric past and involve the actions of gods and supernatural beings. Legends are set in the historic past, involve human protagonists, and call for an element of belief or disbelief. Folktales are set in the historic past, may involve human or nonhuman characters, are fictional, and are told primarily for entertainment, although they may be used to point out a moral or illustrate a truth. Except among Indian tribes in the region, myths are not found in Ozark folk tradition.

Legends of the supernatural are very common in the Ozarks, and one of the most popular, as it is elsewhere in America, is the story of the vanishing hitchhiker. Usually, as in the following three variants, this legend is presented as a true happening, though not as a personal experience of the narrator:

I heard this story a long, long time ago, I don't remember exactly when it was that I first heard it. This girl, named Laura Starr, and her boyfriend were on their way to their senior prom and had a terrible wreck. They were both killed. Oh, I forgot to tell you that this happened on a Friday night, and it was raining really hard and storming. Anyway, they were both killed and if you drive by the London cemetery on a rainy Friday night then you can see her on the side of the road trying to get a ride with someone. Some people even say that they have picked her up and gave her a ride and then she'll just disappear.[1]

I've heard this story since I was very young, I first heard it from my grandmother. There was a girl named Laura Starr, and on her wedding night she and her husband were on their way to their honeymoon, and they were involved in a bad accident. There was a storm at the time of the accident and supposedly if you drive by the London cemetery (where the girl is buried) on certain nights you can see her on the side of the road. Some say she is wanting a ride to go in search of her husband, who was also killed in the accident. Her tombstone in the cemetery is inscribed with "Gentle stranger passing by, as you are so once was I, As I am so you shall be, So prepare to follow me."[2]

I've heard this tale for as long back as I can remember. Supposedly there was a couple who, after they were married and were on their way to their reception were involved in a one-car accident which resulted in the deaths of both of them. Rumor has it that if you drive by on certain nights you can see her trying to get a ride with someone.[3]

Not all supernatural legends involve ghosts; sometimes real objects take on eerie qualities:

There is a cemetery within walking distance of where I used to live. It had a lot of trees in it and some of them looked funny. They were strange-shaped. I have heard stories about cemeteries all my life but you know how you hear something like ghost stories and make fun of it. I even heard this tale by my mother and dad but had forgotten it until my experience. Here's what happened to me that night.

I was walking home from visiting a friend and it was getting to be pretty late. I got close to the cemetery and it got darker about that time. I don't know whether I imagined it or it really happened though. Anyway I looked up at this old tree there by the cemetery's gate and it was kind of hazy around the top of it. I thought at first someone might have been burning trash or something and the smoke had collected up there, but I didn't see or smell anyone burning anything.

While I was looking at the tree it started moving and twisting around like it would probably look if it was during a tornado. The wind was blowing but not as hard down where I was standing to make a tree do that. No normal wind could. I was so scared I ran all the way home. My grandmother had told me later that the tree was supposed to be haunted by a spirit of a poor man who had bad luck all his life. I can't explain what happened about the tree. I just know it was strange, one of the strangest experiences I've ever had.[4]

Many of the legends that circulate in Ozark communities deal with local characters. As in the following examples, the people in such stories are rarely noted for their brilliance but more often for their naivete or ignorance:

My sister stayed with me when I had the store and she baked doughnuts and brought them over there. And she said, "Now, Stocky, you can have one of these doughnuts but you can't eat the hole."

And we watched him, he was eating all around that. Finally, he looked up at Marie and said, "How in hell can I keep from eating this hole?"[5]

This old man went to homestead forty acres of land. Well, he went to the courthouse and got in there and, of course, they had to have the information about where it was at. This guy said to him, he said, "Well, sir, what township and section is that land in?"

The old man he looked at him and said, "They ain't no township and section to it." He said, "The range is fine. They's peavines and beggar lice waist deep around the door."[6]

One time we was over here at Marshall, a bunch of us boys, went in to eat breakfast. An old boy we used to have a lot of fun out of him. We got in there to eat breakfast and we ordered bacon and eggs. Of course, they come around and asked this old boy, "How do you want your eggs cooked?"

He said, "Well, just put 'em in the pan with some grease and fry 'em."[7]

Another old guy around here goin' to Kansas one time, got up there in Kansas and they used to have tokens for sales tax. Well, we got up there and these boys, some of 'em, had to have some beer. This old man was religious and they all eat breakfast, some of 'em had beer and he didn't, you know. And he got up there to pay for his meal. He asked that girl how much he owed her. She put it down there and she said, "Do you have a token, mister?"

He said, "No thanks, lady, I don't drink."[8]

Local characters also become legendary for their drunkenness, their strength, their mooching, and numerous other traits and characteristics:

A fellow got drunk one time way back yonder. I ain't going to call his name. He got drunk and I reckon he got so drunk he didn't know where he was at. And he went home and he come to the door and he knocked on the door and his wife come to the door and called him by name and said, "Come on in."

"Well," he said, "well, I'd just as well, my wife will run me off when I get home anyway."[9]

I heard dad tell about Steve Treat. One time somebody had run a wheel off of a wagon. And they had some prize poles trying to prize it up. Said that old man come along. He looked around there and he said, "Boy, let me get under there and you'ns get your wheel. I'll raise it up and you'ns pull it off."

They said they thought, "He'll play thunder a-raising that up."

Said he got under there, put his hands on his knees and went to straightening up and raised up and they put the wheel on it.[10]

This boy was always smoking, you know. I used to smoke and he was always bumming me for a smoke. I was coming up the road and I had my can nearly empty and I had another new one and I seen a little old snake going across the road so I just caught that little old snake and put it in that can. I went on up there and he said, "If you ain't got no Prince Albert I'll take Velvet." He said, "I'd take a ready roll if you had it."

I said, "No, here's some in this can."

He said, "Let me have it." He opened it up and run his finger down in there and that snake run out of there. He throwed that down and I never heard such a jabbering.

I said, "Here, you want some of this?"

He said, "No, no."

He never would bum from me no more.[11]

Sometimes yarns generally told as fictions get attached to local characters. Employing a technique found in Boccaccio's *Decameron* and numerous other sources, the following tale has been attributed to Mark Twain, as well as to at least one less famous Ozark resident. In fictional renderings it is usually told as an experience of the narrator. Because this version relates it as the true experience of a person in the community, the informant chose not to name the person involved.

An old boy back over here had been hunting and he was a-walking down the road. He had his old shotgun and he had his old hound. He was walking down the road and the game warden came along and picked him up. He didn't know him and he didn't know the game warden, see. He asked him if he wanted a ride and he said, "Yeh." So he just throwed his old hound up in the back of the pickup and got in with the game warden.

Going down the road he told the game warden about all the hunting he had done that day. Directly the game warden asked him his name and he told him. So he asked the game warden and he told him. So, they went on down the road a little bit. Directly he said to this fellow, "You didn't know I was the game warden of this county did you?"

He said, "No, I thought you said you were so-and-so."

He said, "No, I'm the game warden from over here at Mountain Home."

This old boy said, "Well, you don't know who you're a-talking to either, do you?"

He said, "Well, you told me so-and-so was your name."

He said, "You're talking to the biggest damn liar in this country." He said, "That dog won't run a thing in the world back there."[12]

Many Ozark legends deal with important historical events, such as the Civil War. Rather than focus on major battles, these narratives emphasize matters of more immediate interest to the narrators, such as how one's family coped with the hardships of war:

Grandmother said one time they was some Union soldiers came there, 'n they were takin' everythin', ya know, 'n one young Yankee soldier was out grabbin' some Irish potatoes in the garden. 'N she went out there. She said to that young soldier, "Aren't you ashamed a' yourself, young man? I'm jus' like a widder here, with my children. That's all we have ta eat." She said, "Don't you know you'll have ta die some day, you're liable to git killed in the War anytime?"

He said, "I realize that, good woman, and I hope to meet you in a better world, but right now I'm very hungry, 'n I must have these potatoes."[13]

My mother she had five brothers and sisters and then she had six cousins and their mothers lived together. I think there was about fourteen in the family but their husbands had gone to the army. So, they had an old cow that would come in every evening. She said it just seemed like she knew that they needed her or something. She'd come in every evening and they'd milk her and she'd just go right back to the woods. And that's all that kept her and her family a-going for a long time. That was the saver of their lives.[14]

My grandfather Rorie he was in the army and he said that they was so hungry that this little old male hog, just as poor as you ever see one, a razorback they call it. He said we was so hungry we just got down off the horses, two of us, one held the little old pig and the other one killed him and cut out the ham and we eat that because we was starving to death.[15]

My grandfather Hezekiah Rose was in the Civil War. One time they run out of food and was about to starve to death. Then they had a little old mule just as fat as it could be and they decided they'd kill that little old mule and eat it. They did but he said he couldn't eat it to save his life. The more he chewed on it the bigger it got.[16]

Historical legends concerning the Civil War invariably include jay-hawker stories. The word "jayhawker" originally applied to a group of antislavery guerrilla fighters on the Kansas-Missouri border who were later incorporated into the Union Army. This group was notorious for burnings and killings, and eventually Confederate propagandists labeled any Union sentiment in Confederate states such as Arkansas as the result of jayhawkers. History books today generally refer to Union raiders as jayhawkers and to Confederate raiders as bushwhackers. The hillfolk make no such careful distinctions; to them the guerrillas who specialized in terrorizing those left at home during the war were usually called jay-hawkers. Even today most informants regard these raiders as thugs or deserters who were taking advantage of the Civil War to enrich them-selves.

Typically, jayhawker narratives describe the raiders barging in on someone, often an ancestor of the narrator or someone who has the narra-tor's sympathy and who is minding his own business:

My great-grandfather fought in the Civil War and my great-grandmother lived alone with the children and my grandpa was just a little boy about eight or ten years old. And they had a colored woman, a black woman, that stayed with them and helped 'em work. Everytime they'd get in good shape here'd come the jayhawkers and take everything away from them, kill all their ducks and geese, and everything. One day they came in and they thought my great-grandmother she had gold and silver and they wanted that, see. They was going to burn her house down so they turned the featherbed back. One told the other one to set it afire. He said, "No, what about us just killing so-and-so boy?"

And they got him and took him outside and told him to climb up on the fence, get up behind them. So they got their horses and come around to pick him up. Instead of him climbing up on the fence there was a cornfield and went up there and laid down in the grass. And they hunted for him and went back. When my great-grandmother decided it was safe for him to come back she come in and hollered for him.[17]

In Ozark legends jayhawkers generally take any food or valuables in the house. Sometimes they torture or kill a male member of the household to make the other family members reveal the hiding place of a treasure. The following jayhawker story deviates from the norm in that a baby is substituted for the usual adult male sacrifice, and the death is a result of sadism rather than of an attempt to force the revelation of a hidden treasure:

Some woman had a little baby born and it was some of my kinfolk but I don't know what relation it was, but it was tollible close to my kin. And the jayhawkers come in and they was just going to kill the whole bunch. Well, the mothers kept a-begging and a-pleading for them to leave the children alone and trying to get them to take them instead. And they said, "Well, if you'll just give me that little newborn baby we'll let the rest go."

They knew that that was all that would save 'em and at last they give up to let them take the little baby. And they took their shoelaces and tied them around that baby's head and tied it to one of the horse's tails. It was a-goin' up the road, they was a rider got on the horse and rode off with it, and it just a-flopping, of course, just whipped it all to pieces. That was the most evil story I heard of mama telling but I used to hear her tell a lot of them.[18]

Often in the stories, jayhawkers destroy any valuables they can't take with them. The following is a rare account in which the person under attack gets the best of the jayhawkers:

This woman the army got her husband she was left with three little children. They were around there a few days and they heard a wagon come down the hill. They lived on top of a bluff at the end of a road. She told her children just be quiet and she'd slip around with her gun. They come in and looked through the house and got all they wanted. Then they went outside and got the team and got the wagon and filled it full of corn. Said when they started back up there on the curve on the road she shot the man in the wagon that had their team. That scared the team and they whirled and started running back. The people in the other wagon they went on, they was afraid they'd get hurt.

Said they left that man all day up there and nobody come. They talked about it wondering what they was going to do with him. They drug him down to the bluff and throwed him over the big bluff. That's all they could do. I reckon that happened over here at Culp. I heard it did.[19]

Even rarer is an episode in which the jayhawkers are helped by those they attack:

My grandfather's sister, Patsy, lived down somewhere in the neighborhood of where Long Creek runs into Big Creek. Jayhawkers come in on them there one night and they said she walked plumb from over there into Big Flat, she had a lot of relatives here in Big Flat, and told them about the gangs of 'em being there.

They was a bunch of men from here went over there and the main leader of the bunch they was interested in him not being killed. After these people come, I suppose there was men and women too from the way they told it, they dressed the main leader up in women's clothes, put a bonnet on him. Two women, one got on each side of him, and, of course, the ones who went to kill 'em they didn't know this. And they come leading this old man out with that old woman's clothes and bonnet on and that saved his life. They thought he was an old woman and he got away. But they killed some of the jayhawkers, I don't know just how many. But that old main leader got away on them dressing him up like an old woman.[20]

This type of clever escape is a motif that is found in folk literature around the world. In tales from Iceland and from Italy, for example, a husband disguises himself as a woman in order to spy on his wife who he believes is unfaithful to him. In other Italian tales, a boy disguises himself as a woman to embarrass a priest. Several Lithuanian and Russian narratives feature a man disguising himself as a woman in order to take the bride's place at a wedding feast. There are many other variations on this theme but most differ from the Ozark legend in that they are told as fiction rather than as an account of an actual happening. These same motifs are used in some Ozark legends to describe how Ozark residents escaped the jayhawkers:

I think I can remember the man, Dave Perry. He lived out south a' here near a place called Metalton. But anyway, it was a Perry; if it wasn't Dave Perry, it was from that family, I'm sure.

He was home, as was a common thing fer the soldiers in Civil War days. He was home fer a period of time. 'N he knew it was not safe for him t' be there because someone might kill him, because to weaken the South they'd quite often kill the able-bodied men who were left home, whether they were the right age to serve in the army or not. It may be a teenage boy—they'd kill him sometime— that'd happen.

But he realized he might be in trouble. An' one day while he was home on this furlough or this period of time that he'd spend with the family—he looked out the front a' the house 'n saw some men comin', gallopin' on their horses.

Well, he knew if he crawled under the bed 'er went upstairs, 'er went in any part a' the house he'd likely be located. He knew if he went out the back door he'd be in view a' these people.

So he saw his sister's dress and bonnet hangin' on the headboard of the bed. So he put them on as rapidly as he could, 'n picked up the water bucket as though he planned to go to the spring fer a bucket a' water.

He went to the spring, 'n they followed—the family followed him that far, but they didn't find him. But they did find the bucket, the bonnet, and the dress left at the spring; so they jest assumed that he went over the hill.[21]

Accounts of how people escaped jayhawkers are common; frequently the narratives, while very exciting, are implausible:

Ananias Horton was my uncle and he was in the army and the jayhawkers caught him and put him in an old house with three, four, or five more in with him. The watchman went to sleep that night and Ananias raised that door up and crawled out. The jayhawkers took in after him and they was getting close to him so he found an old hollow log and he crawled up in that hollow log. Them jayhawkers just jumped that old log and went on.[22]

While most Civil War and jayhawker stories are family narratives, they are far from being the only type of family tales. Another popular type of family yarn involves hidden treasure:

Well, my great-grandfather, Ben Hancock, when he come from Tennessee he settled in Boone County, south of Harrison 'bout five mile. But, of course, Harrison wasn't there at that time. But anyway, that's where he first settled.

He come into this country, a' course, y' might say, with nothin'. He didn't have a place to live or anything until he built him a place. So he built him a log cabin, moves in it, an' then a' course, the first thing he had to do was to go clear him up some ground to raise food.

So, he went to clearin' ground, makin' rails, fenced 'im a little place there to grow him some food—corn 'n what have ya.

They was a rock layin' there—a big flat stone. An' he noticed that in particular when he moved it, because it had a corn tassle cut on it. An' he looked at that, 'n got pretty well—y' know—how it was layin' before he moves it. So he takes it outta the field, a' course, throws it over in the corner a' the fence.

So, after he gits his ground all cleaned up, why one day he was at the house, 'n he seen someone down the field. An' he watched 'em a little while, 'n he seen that he was a' lookin' for somethin'. He was a' lookin' round all over that field, there.

So after awhile he takes a notion to go down to see what he was lookin' for. So he goes down. He could see it was a Indian, alright.

'N he asked 'im what he was lookin' for, 'n if he could be any help to 'im.

So he told 'im, he says, "When you cleaned this ground here," said, "did you find a rock with a corn tassle cut on it?"

He says, "I did."

He said, "Do you know where it's at?"

He said, "Yessir," says, "it's down there at the corner a' the fence."

He says, "Could you git that rock 'n lay it back," he says, "approximately like it was layin?" He says, "That's our guide," says, "that's all we got to go by to travel."

'N he says, "Yes, I kin get it, 'n put it jest about I think like it was."

So he goes 'n gits the rock, 'n they was talkin'. So this Indian, he tells 'im, says, "If you white men know what the Indians know," says, "you could shoe yer horses with silver 'n gold."

'N he says, "If you would let me blindfold you," he says, "I would take you to this, 'n show you this silver 'n gold. It's in a cave in a mountain back there." He says, "I would blindfold ya," says, "I would take the blindfold off when we get there, 'n let you see it. Then I'll blindfold ya, 'n bring ya back home."

Course at that time the white man 'n the Indian wadn't gittin' along too well, b'cause the white man had drove 'em outta the country. So, my grandfather, he didn't wanta take the chance, so he wouldn't go with 'im.

But he come on in towards the Sulphur—to what we call the Sulphur Mountain south of Harrison—in there—into the mountains. 'N my grandfather then, of course, never did see him anymore; never did know what happened to 'im.

But if they was silver 'n gold in there, it's never been found yet.

You see, that's where he was at. He didn't know whether to believe the Indian 'r not: whether that was actually so about the silver 'n gold, 'r whether he was jes a-tellin' this to git 'im to go with 'im—git 'im off, y' know, ta git rid of 'im.

So, he wouldn't go along.[23]

One other type of historical legendry that is popular with Ozarkers, particularly those living in communities with unusual names is place name legends. These come into being because people have a need for explanation, and because sometimes, as in the case of Big Flat, Arkansas, the conventional historical record says nothing about how the community received its name.

I have heard that the first post office that was ever here was called Big Yellow Flat but I've never seen anything on that. I wouldn't say that's right. Some people asked 'em why and they said well, they couldn't figure out why unless—it's surrounded by gravel land all of it and this right through here is kind of a clay, sandy land until you go down here a little ways and there's gravel.[24]

They said how come Big Flat to get its name was from this spring, it was just a big spring. People then didn't have modern houses they had to go to where there was a spring or a creek to get their water. And they said it was named Big Flat because it was just flat. And it was called the Big Flat Spring. Uncle Ike Rose deeded this land where the spring is but, you see, that was a community spring for a long time. But they finally got where they'd get into it about it.[25]

In addition to historical legends, there are many Ozark legends that deal with supposed events of more recent occurrence. Particularly appealing, especially to parents of small children, are contemporary legends like the following:

I heard that a little girl was kidnapped in Wal-Mart or K-Mart last summer. A man came and grabbed her from her mother when her back was turned. When her mom heard her screaming she ran to the front and got the manager. He guarded the front door and the mother and workers searched the store. Her mom found her in the men's bathroom with different clothes on and her hair cut off. The man that took the girl tried to run out of the store and the police caught him.[26]

All I know is that it was at Wal-Mart a couple of years ago and that this lady was shopping with her little girl, I think. I think she was in a stroller, I'm not really sure. The mom turned around and the baby was gone. The person that took it took it to a bathroom. They had bought some different clothes for it and took it to a bathroom and shaved its head. I think the baby was eighteen months old, so it was little, you know, and dressed it up as a little boy. The mom went to get security and they caught him. I'm not even sure it was a man or a woman. That's all I heard.[27]

I remember it being in the Venture Store in Fort Smith. I think I saw it on the channel 5 news. It was about a little girl who got away from her mother, the mother reacted by locking all the doors, so that no one could get away. They found the little girl in the bathroom with her hair cut off and in a change of clothes and her hair up under a hat or something like that and they caught her.[28]

It is evident that some legends are told without any thought of entertainment but are offered by their narrators as facts or news. Others, however, such as legends about the supernatural, are told as much for their entertainment value as for their purported factual aspects.

In the Ozarks, as in the rest of the United States, the most popular folktales are not the relatively complicated fairy tales popularly associated with children's literature. This is not to suggest that no one tells such narratives any longer, only that they are infrequently encountered. Perhaps they always were less popular than is often believed. Far more common were such tales as the following, an example of a "catch" tale, which appears in *The Journal of Marian Tebbetts Banes*. Banes called it a favorite with children in Washington County, Arkansas, during the antebellum era:

An old woman
All skin and Bo-o-ones (groan)
One day she thought to church she'd stray.

To hear the preacher sing and pray (groan)
And when she got to the church stile,
She thought she'd rest a little while (groan)
And when she got to the church door
She thought she'd rest a little more (groan)
And when she got to the church within
She heard the people pray and sing (groan)
She looked up, she looked down
She saw a corpse laid on the ground (prolonged groan)
The woman to the parson said
Will I look so when I am dead?
The parson to the woman said
You will look so . . .
A yell and shout and much consternation among the intent listeners.
Much depends on the narrator and the ability to do some good groaning in telling the story (p. 67).

Banes also said that "Pull Me Out Simon," which she called an "Uncle Remus story," was a favorite in her family. Her "Uncle Remus" was John Dixon, a black man who was a blacksmith. Banes admitted that part of the story's popularity was due to Dixon's manner of telling:

There was one story that especially held the children and made them thoughtful, that of Simon, the bad boy who went fishing on Sunday against his mother's wishes. That was so dramatically told that one could almost see the boy, obeying the demands of the terrible thing he hauled in from the water. After a big tug at the line, he heard a voice say:

"Pull me out, Simon,
Pull me out, Simon,
Pull me out, Simon, hi week a day!"

"And," said John, thunderstruck, "Simon pulled him out."

One could almost see the impossible thing, squirming on the ground, from the horror on John's face, and his backing away from the place his eyes were fixed on.

"Now, take me home, Simon,
Take me home, Simon,
Take me home, Simon, hi week a day!"

"And Simon tuck him home," with terrible dismay on his face.

"Cut me up, Simon,
Cut me up, Simon,
Cut me up, Simon, hi week a day!"

"And Simon cut him up." Solemnly, shaking his head.

"Put me in the pot, Simon,
Put me in the pot, Simon,

Put me in the pot, Simon, hi week a day!"
"And Simon put him in the pot."
"Cook me good and done, Simon,
Cook me good and done, Simon,
Cook me good and done, Simon, hi week a day!"
"And Simon cooked him good and done"—eyes rolling and voice trembling.
"Now, eat me up, Simon,
Eat me up, Simon,
Eat me up, Simon, hi week a day!"
"And Simon et him all up—he didn't leave narry a bone."
"Now you'll bust wide open, Simon,
You'll bust wide open, Simon,
You'll bust wide open, Simon, hi week a day!"
"And Simon busted," horror stricken, "and the devil jumped out, laughing and wiggling his tail, and ran off," said John as he stepped aside, out of the way, to let the devil pass (in *The Journal of Marian Tebbetts Banes*, pp. 66–67. Baughman's motif Q223.6.3 "Punishment for fishing on Sunday" applies.)

Such narratives are still told, but they are generally reserved for children, who were, even in Banes's day, their primary audience. Now they are much less in demand than tall tales. Among these "big stories," as they are frequently called, none are more popular than those about fantastic insects such as mosquitos or ticks. A common yarn of this type is given here in three versions, the first from the 1930s, the second from the 1970s, and the third from the 1980s:

Another well-known Ozark "windy" is a tale of the lumber-camps, and concerns a yoke of oxen called Tom and Jerry. Both animals "showed up missin' " one morning, and several men set out to search for them. Jerry was soon located, but Tom was nowhere to be found. Tom always wore a bell, and finally the bell was heard on a distant ridge. When the loggers reached the spot they were dumfounded to hear the tinkling of the bell directly over their heads. On looking up they saw "a turrible big skeeter, big as one o' these hyar airplanes they got nowadays, a-settin' on top of a big pine." Looking closer, they saw that he was picking his teeth with one of Tom's horns. "He'd done et pore Tom plumb up, an' thar he set a-ringing' th' bell for Jerry!" (in *Ozark Mountain Folks* pp. 158–159).

I was down in Louisiana. I went off down through ther, 'n I hired out to a farmer down ther ta work.
I'd been ther 'bout two-three days, 'n he told me, he said, "I want ya to go out ta th' back a' the pasture 'n drive my milk cows." He said, "They'll be right 'n the back a' the pasture."
'N I said, "Well, how many cows ya got over there?"

"Oh," he said, "I've got fifteen er twenty," but said, "I only want her—the milk cow drove up." Says, "You'll know 'er, she's got a bell on."

I said, "Alright." So I walked back there, 'n I walked about a half a mile, 'n I stopped 'n listened, 'n I couldn't hear the bell ringin'. I went on back, 'n after awhile I spotted a bunch a' cattle back over ther, under some shade trees.

So I took out, 'n b'fore I got over ther the bell quit ringin'.

I walked on up to them cattle. I couldn't see no cow with a bell on; 'n I couldn't hear it ringin'. 'N after awhile this bell started ta ringin' over ta one side, 'n I looked around ther—'n the mosquitoes had ate this cow up, 'n was standin' ther ringin' the bell fer the calf ta come.[29]

An old man one time said way back there before they went to dipping these cattle the ticks got so bad. And he said he had an old cow to come up missing. He said he got out looking for her and he could just hear the bell a-rattling, and a-rattling, and he kept a-looking and hunting. He said he got down there and it was one of these big old speck backed ticks had eat the cow up and was up on the stump a-rattling the bell a-looking for the calf to come. He wanted to eat it up.[30]

Also very popular is the following narrative about the effects of a snakebite on a piece of wood:

My Uncle John went fishing a long time ago in the Buffalo River and there was this big water moccasin come up on him. He got scared and started to hit him with his oar and that water moccasin bit his oar and that oar started swelling till it stopped up the Buffalo River. It took twenty mules to pull it out of there. Uncle John took it to the sawmill and sawed it up and built him a huge house out of it. My Aunt Nattie she went to paint it one day and she mixed some turpentine up with the paint. That turpentine must have took the swelling out of it for now it ain't nothing but a bird house.[31]

Many tales of absurd ignorance involving local characters are found in the Ozark folktale repertoire. One of the most popular is recounted here by a twelve-year-old informant:

Back when grandpa was a little boy they lived in the country and they'd never seen a banana before. They got to town and some of his friends got a job herding cattle. They got 'em up on this train and they seen this guy selling fruit. They said, "Let's try one of these funny shaped fruit."

So they bought one and they didn't know how to get it open. They watched a man up front and then finally got it open and nobody would take the first bite. They said, "Well, since grandpa's the oldest he'll take the first bite."

They was coming up on this tunnel where it got pitch black. Grandpa was just about to put his teeth into it and when he did they went in that tunnel. Grandpa said, "Lordy boys, don't take a bite out of her. It'll make you blind as a bat."[32]

Other favorite themes include laziness and lying:

Oh, this guy, he had a family, 'n he wouldn't work. 'N his wife 'n kids had ta do all the work, 'n he jes wouldn't work.

He said, naw he wouldn't work—he wasn't able ta work. Well, the neighbors around would give 'em stuff, 'n hep 'em out.

'N finally they got tired of it. 'N they told 'em, said, "Now, John, we've been heppin' you 'bout two-three years now. Now, we gittin tired of it. Now you're gonna either go to work, or we gonna bury you alive."

So, it went on fer 'bout a month.

One day this guy was comin' from town, 'n they met a wagon with a casket in it. 'N he stopped 'em, 'n said, "Well, who's daid?"

"Oh," they said, "ain't nobody daid." But said, "Y' know John, he won't work 'n support his family. 'N we been tellin' 'im what we gonna do." 'N said, "We gonna bury 'im alive."

"Oh," he said, "I wouldn't do that if I were you guys."

He said, "I've got some corn at the house that I'll give 'im. 'N he kin take it to the mill 'n have it ground. 'N he'll have some cornbread, 'n somebody will give 'im milk."

'N this John, he raised up in the casket. He said, "Is that corn shelled?"

'N this guy said, "No."

'N he said, "Well, drive on."[33]

You know, Uncle Will did have a running contest with Lyin' Frank Carlton. An' there'd always be something that they would be pulling on each other.

So the boys around the square, an' the post office, an' the bank, decided that it'd be a nice thing, an' be very interesting to git those two men together an' let 'em have a contest to see which could tell the biggest lie.

So, they finally got them to agree to meet an' have the contest. An' they met on the north side a' the square at the post office—which was on the north side then.

They was a sheriff there, an' the postmaster, an' all the officers from the courthouse, an' the bank—they all lined up there.

Mr. Carlton was there an' Uncle Will didn't show up.

So they began to git a li'l uneasy. An' so—finally they looked up the street, an' there coming down by the bank was Uncle Will—n' he was walking, swinging his arms, an' stepping out like he was walking fer wages.

He came right down by where they were; walked right on by—didn't even look at 'em.

And he got jes by them, "Why, What in the?! . . . Hey! Hey, Will, aren't you gonna stop?"

He turned around and looked at 'em. "Did you hear that Bud Riggs fell in his saw and got cut all to pieces?"

Lying Frank Carlton, he said, "Oh, my God, he's one of my best friends."

He lit out running, 'n ran all the way down Springtown.

Got down there: Bud Riggs 'as setting on the porch whittling.

That ended the matter.[34]

Animals and fish crop up in a number of Ozark folktales, although usually as essential nonspeaking figures rather than as the talking animals found in narratives such as "Tar Baby."

This here worker went up to this guy's house and he asked him if he had a drink. He said, "There's a spring out there in the back. There's a gourd hanging up there on a bush that you can use for a dipper."

He started out through there and he met this old turtle coming up. Then he ran back to the house and said, "Hey, mister, your spring's running dry. I seen your dipper walking home."[35]

Once there was this man who loved to fish. One time he started to fish in a pond where there was a catfish no one could ever catch. So he got his fishing pole and started over to it and when he got there the fish almost pulled him in. He got so mad because it hauled off his line but he went back and caught that ole fish. But it had so many hooks in its mouth he sold it for scrap iron.[36]

Yeah, they had a fox hunt.

'N they come from Tennessee, Missouri, Kentucky, 'n ev'rywhar up above Evening Shade ther'.

'N they was a doctor up ther by the name a' Dr. Tibbles, 'n he had a couple a' fox dogs. 'N they were really good dogs, 'n tellin' how fast they was. 'N Doc Tibbles set ther, 'n he never said nothin'.

So finally some guy said, "Doc," said, "you've never said nothin' 'bout your dogs," said, "how fast is yore dogs?"

"Aw," he said, "these dogs that I've got now is good dogs, but," he said, "they nothin' like I used to have."

He said, "I had a dog one time—that was the fastest dog I ever seen."

He said, "We was out on a fox hunt." 'N he said, "We jumped this fox." 'N he said, "He run fer about a half a' mile, 'n he was jes fixin' ta ketch that fox," 'n he said, "he slowed down jest a littl' ta grab the fox, 'n the fox whirled 'n went ta the left right quick."

'N he said, "The dog was goin' so fast that he couldn't stop." 'N he said, "They was a steel post there. 'N he hit that steel post," 'n said, "jest split that dog right half in two."

'N he said, "I happened ta be a-standin' ther about ten steps," 'n he said, "I run 'n grabbed that dog 'n sewed 'im back up."

'N said, "I put two feet up, 'n two feet down," 'n said, "That dog would outrun ever' dog in the country. He'd run awhile on two feet, 'n flop over on the other two feet." 'N said, "He outrun ever' dog in that whole country."[37]

The Ozark Folk Center

Unlike most other American mountain regions, the Ozarks has a large center devoted to the study and presentation of its culture. The Ozark Folk Center, situated on four hundred acres (of which eighty are developed), is probably also the largest facility in the country concerned with the traditional culture of a particular region. It therefore seems worthwhile to give a brief history of this institution.

In a sense, the idea for the Ozark Folk Center had its beginnings in the 1920s. Many people were distressed with certain cultural events taking place during the Jazz Age and thought that America would be better off if it returned to the ways of earlier, simpler times. To people such as Henry Ford, jazz was an abomination that needed to be replaced by traditional American music. Toward this end, Ford sponsored fiddle contests, an old-time dance orchestra, and other similar events. It was during this time that a variety of programs such as radio barn dances (the National Barn Dance in 1924 and the Grand Ole Opry in 1925, to cite the two most famous examples) were started.

Also in those years a number of folk festivals began to be held, some of which have endured to the present. The Mountain Dance and Folk Festival that was started in Asheville, North Carolina, in 1928 by Bascom Lamar Lunsford is still going strong as it nears its seventieth year. Almost as long-lived is the National Folk Festival that Sarah Gertrude Knott established in St. Louis in 1934. This particular festival has been important because instead of presenting a program that represented only the dominant culture as many of the others did, Knott employed a multicultural approach that offered a more accurate picture of the nation's diversity.

By no means were these festivals without flaws; indeed, they frequently offered a presentation of culture that was not only excessively romantic and nostalgic but that was aseptic and never actually existed. Nevertheless, they were very popular and for a time many colleges and communities throughout America had their own folk festivals. Thus, St. Joe, Arkansas, a tiny community between Marshall and Harrison, started

Aerial view, Ozark Folk
Center (Photo courtesy
Ozark Folk Center)

such a festival in the late 1930s. The idea also appealed to people in nearby Stone County, Arkansas, but their first festival, held in August of 1941, was destined to be the last for more than two decades. The United States entered World War Two in December of that year and for the next four years people had more important things on their minds than folk festivals.

The concept of holding an annual festival never really died, and it resurfaced again in the early 1960s. By that time the Ozark Foothills Handicraft Guild had been established to help Ozark residents, particularly those in Stone County, improve their lives economically; traditional crafts were regarded as one means of achieving that goal. Thus, a craft show was held on the courthouse square in Mountain View, the county seat of Stone County, and proved successful enough to encourage its promoters to try it again the following year. Recalling the 1941 festival, which focused primarily on music, those in charge decided that the addition of traditional music might help boost the crowds. The guild didn't have to look far for musicians. For some time Lloyd Hollister, a doctor in Mountain View, had been having informal music gatherings in his office on weekends. The musicians agreed to perform at the second crafts show, an event that marked the beginning of the Arkansas Folk Festival, which still continues. The name is actually slightly misleading because,

Famous Ozark folk-
singer, Booth Campbell,
performing at 1941 folk
festival (Photo courtesy
Ozark Folk Center)

with a few exceptions, the festival has always been essentially a showcase
for folk musicians, dancers, and singers from Stone County and the counties immediately surrounding it.

This festival was not an isolated event. By the late 1950s the so-called
folksong revival was in full swing. Considered to have begun in 1958
when the Kingston Trio did a very untraditional recording of "Tom
Dooley," it lasted approximately a decade. Basically a reaction to rock 'n'
roll, just as in the 1920s similar music arose in response to jazz, the revival spawned a multitude of folk festivals, many of which were more
festival than folk. Most of these events, including several in other parts
of Arkansas, have long since passed into history, with the Arkansas Folk
Festival being one of the notable exceptions.

Within a few years the festival in Mountain View had become successful beyond initial expectations. It also surpassed the town's ability to ac-
commodate the event. Every available spot, including the high school
gym, was given over to the April festival; it began to be spread out over
three weekends because of the huge crowds. However, what was really
needed was a permanent facility that would house the festival. At this
point, John Opitz, head of the Arkansas Office of Economic Opportunity,
hit upon the idea of a folk center. Actually, Opitz had more in mind than

merely housing the annual festival. The city of Mountain View had no water system then, and, because of the way certain federal granting regulations were structured, a community that was proposing a good project would also become eligible for funds for ancillary projects, such as water systems. Opitz convinced many local people that this was a good idea, and in the mid-1960s interested parties from Stone County began making presentations in favor of an Ozark folk center to legislators in Washington, D. C.

The original concept of the folk center was somewhat different from the one envisioned by the organization that actually opened the facility. Initially the center was to be a school where persons from throughout the Ozarks could come and learn traditional craft skills. They were then expected to return to their home communities and to earn at least a portion of their income practicing what they had learned in Mountain View. The shops where individual craftsmen now demonstrate their techniques for visitors were intended to be classrooms. The present restaurant was to serve as the school's cafeteria and the lodge as its dormitory. This is not quite how the project turned out.

The proposal for the folk center came at a fortuitous time because the government's War on Poverty had been recently undertaken. In terms of per capita income, the second poorest county in Arkansas was Stone, while the poorest was its neighbor, Izard. Thus, the proposed center was ideally located to get War on Poverty funding. Also, Wilbur Mills was in a position of prominence and had a great deal to say about how and where federal funds were spent. He saw little reason to object to funneling several million dollars into his home state, especially when the place receiving the money was so ideal from the War on Poverty perspective. As a result, the city of Mountain View was awarded a grant of 3.4 million dollars on an 80–20 basis. This meant that 20 percent of the total had to be repaid over a fifty-year period beginning in the late 1960s.

The city of Mountain View sought bids from companies capable of building a folk center. Advance Projects, from New York City, won the bid, but, after getting about 75 percent of the facility completed, it went bankrupt. When the bidding process was reinaugurated, the Arkansas Department of Parks and Tourism won. While they did not actually have disdain for the original plan, they did have some practical matters to consider. Certain groups in state government were less than enthusiastic about the state taking over the folk center, feeling that it was just another money-losing proposition, so Parks and Tourism would have to take steps to make sure their new park didn't become a financial burden. When viewed in this light, the crafts school didn't look like a good idea because it had no real source of income beyond a small sales shop, which didn't seem sufficient to support such a large facility. Therefore, it was decided that converting the folk center into an outdoor museum would make better financial sense. This would mean that not only would the craft products, recordings of music, books, and similar items that were sold in the sales shop be sources of revenue, but that tickets to craft and music programs and a restaurant and lodge would also give the center a continuing source of income.

So, the folk center opened in 1973 as an outdoor museum featuring traditional Ozark crafts and music. Initially, contracts were made with the Ozark Foothills Handicraft Guild for crafts and with the Rackensack Society, a Mountain View-based gathering of traditional musicians, for music, but within a couple of years this arrangement was dropped in favor of contracts with individual craftsmen and musicians, a method that has been used ever since. Eventually, a crafts director and a music director were added to the staff to handle these portions of the center's programs. In 1976 the first, and to date only, folklorist was hired to serve as a full-time consultant to the center's staff and to head up research.

The Ozark Folk Center has always for the most part had to generate its own revenue, since from the first year it has never received even 10 percent of its annual budget, which is now over 2 million dollars per year, from the state of Arkansas. Still, the original vision of a school has not been entirely discarded. Each year workshops lasting from two days to a week or more are held on various crafts and aspects of music.

CHAPTER FOUR

1. Collected by W. K. McNeil from Jim Rorie, Onia, Arkansas, 1981.

2. Collected by Mary Camron from Della Horton, Big Flat, Arkansas, 1982. Camron, a high school student at the time, called this a ghost story even though there is no mention of a ghost in the text.

3. Collected by W. K. McNeil from George Vickers, Big Flat, Arkansas, 1983.

4. This poem was given to me by Mr. Sherman a few years before his death in the mid-1980s. At the time he told me of the circumstances under which the poem was written and used.

5. Collected by Donna M. Copeland from Zora Arbaugh Moore, Ozone Mountain, Arkansas, January 1988.

6. Collected by Donna M. Copeland from Zora Arbaugh Moore, Ozone Mountain, Arkansas, January 1988.

7. Collected by Donna M. Copeland from Georgia Ann Castile Cowan, Clarksville, Arkansas, June 1968.

8. Collected by Donna M. Copeland from Georgia Ann Castile Cowan, Clarksville, Arkansas, June 1968.

9. Collected by Donna M. Copeland from Zora Arbaugh Moore, Ozone Mountain, Arkansas, January 1988.

10. Collected by Donna M. Copeland from Zora Arbaugh Moore, Ozone Mountain, Arkansas, January 1988.

CHAPTER FIVE

1. Personal letter from Robert Lee "Bob" Wolf, Coffeyville, Kansas, November 29, 1977.

2. Personal letter from Mrs. Dewey R. Yocum, Fredonia, Kansas, March 16, 1977.

3. Personal letter from Madlyn Walters, Jerome, Idaho, March 16, 1978.

4. Personal letter from Robert Lee "Bob" Wolf, Coffeyville, Kansas, November 29, 1977.

5. Personal letter from Robert Lee "Bob" Wolf, Coffeyville, Kansas, November 29, 1977.

6. Personal letter from Landis Deffenbaugh, Willow Springs, Missouri, August 20, 1978.

7. Personal letter from Landis Deffenbaugh, Willow Springs, Missouri, August 20, 1978.

8. Collected by W. K. McNeil from Rance Blankenship, Melbourne, Arkansas, 1979.

9. Collected by W. K. McNeil from the Bob Williams family, Roland, Arkansas, 1986.

10. Collected by W. K. McNeil from Rance Blankenship, Melbourne, Arkansas, 1979.

11. Collected by Theodore Garrison from Mrs. Martha Garrison, Marshall, Arkansas, July 1942. This text was included in Garrison's M. A. thesis at the University of Arkansas, *Forty-Five Folk Songs Collected from Searcy County, Arkansas* (1944), p. 126.

12. Collected by W. K. McNeil from Kenneth Rorie, Batesville, Arkansas, 1979. Rorie learned this, and most of the songs in his repertoire, from his father, Ulis Rorie.

13. Collected by W. K. McNeil from the Bob Williams family, Roland, Arkansas, 1986.

Chapter Six

1. Collected by Eric Lignell from Tim Ryan, Fayetteville, Arkansas, March 1988.

2. Collected by Eric Lignell from Tim Ryan, Fayetteville, Arkansas, March 1988.

3. Collected by Eric Lignell from Greg Kunzelman, Fayetteville, Arkansas, March 1988.

4. Collected by Eric Lignell from Greg Kunzelman, Fayetteville, Arkansas, March 1988.

5. The first text is reported by J. C. Edwards of Webster Groves, Missouri, the second by Mrs. C. H. Turner of Springfield, Missouri, and the third by Mrs. Mahlon J. Hale of Arkadelphia, Arkansas. All three texts appear in *Arkansas Folklore* 2 (May 1952): 2–3.

6. Reported by Teresa Bolinger, Big Flat, Arkansas, 1979, who recalled using the rhyme herself.

7. Reported by Teresa Bolinger, Big Flat, Arkansas, 1979, from her own memory.

8. Reported by Julie Pool, Big Flat, Arkansas, 1979, who recalled using the rhyme herself.

9. Reported by Y. W. Etheridge, Hamburg, Arkansas, in *Arkansas Folklore* 1 (May 1951): 7.

10. Collected by Linda Stevens from Mary Alice Stevens, Big Flat, Arkansas, 1979.

11. Both rhymes were collected by Julie Pool from Russel Pool, Big Flat, Arkansas, 1979.

12. Collected by Mary Camron from Della Horton, Big Flat, Arkansas, 1978.

13. Collected by Nancy Lee from Elma Lee, Big Flat, Arkansas, 1978.

14. Collected by Mary Camron from Della Horton, Big Flat, Arkansas, 1978.

15. All three rhymes were reported by Bradley McCoy, Big Flat, Arkansas, from his own memory.

16. Collected by Mary Camron from Leonard Horton, Big Flat, Arkansas, 1978.

17. Reported by Teresa Bolinger, Big Flat, Arkansas, from her own memory, 1979.

18. Collected by Martin Lee Hafner from Melody Hafner, Big Flat, Arkansas, 1979.

19. Collected by Betty Haddock from Josephine McClanahan, Big Flat, Arkansas, 1979.

20. Collected by Nancy Lee from her mother, Evalee Lee, Big Flat, Arkansas, 1978.

21. Reported by Teresa Bolinger, Big Flat, Arkansas, from her own memory, 1979.

22. Both riddles were collected by Tammy Wynn from Sarah Jane Jarrett, Big Flat, Arkansas, 1979.

23. Both riddles were collected by Kenneth Pemberton from Willie Treat, Big Flat, Arkansas, 1979.

24. Collected by Kenneth Pemberton from Willie Treat, Big Flat, Arkansas, 1979.

25. Both riddles were collected by Kenneth Pemberton from Ira Ballentine, Big Flat, Arkansas, 1979.

26. Collected by Nancy Lee from Willis Lee, Big Flat, Arkansas, 1978.

Chapter Seven

1. Collected by Lee Wilson from Tina Shatwell, age 20, Clarksville, Arkansas, 1988. Ernest W. Baughman, in *Type and Motif Index of the Folktales of England and North America*, assigns the Vanishing Hitchhiker the motif number E332.3.3.1.

2. Collected by Lee Wilson from Kyn Wilcox, age 50, Clarksville, Arkansas, 1988.

3. Collected by Lee Wilson from Emma Vinson, age 57, Clarksville, Arkansas, 1988.

4. Collected by Kristi Rickard from a man identified only as Bill, a former resident of Denning, Arkansas. Unlike many supernatural tales, it is presented as an actual experience of the narrator, although his comments make clear that there is a long-established legend about this tree. Baughman gives no motif that applies to this tale.

5. Collected by W. K. McNeil from Julie Kelley, Big Flat, Arkansas, 1982. Baughman's motifs J1730, "Absurd ignorance," and J1732, "Ignorance of certain foods," apply.

6, 7, 8. All three tales were collected by W. K. McNeil from George Vickers, Big Flat, Arkansas, 1982. Baughman's motif J1730, "Absurd ignorance," applies to all three texts, but there are different nuances in each case. In the first, the humor is based on absurd ignorance of certain legal formalities involved with homesteading. In the second, the humor is based on the main character's failure to comprehend the true meaning of the waitress's question, which, of course, was designed to find out if he wanted his eggs over easy, sunny side up, etc. In the third, the humor is derived from the fact that the protagonist is simply unfamiliar with a practice found in an area outside of his home region. Baughman's motif J1742, "The countryman in the great world," is also appropriate for all three texts.

9, 10, 11. All were collected by W. K. McNeil from George Vickers, Big Flat, Arkansas, 1982. Of course, stories about humorous incidents that occurred while someone was drunk are legion. Baughman's motif X800, "Humor based on drunkenness," is applicable. Possibly such stories are popular in part because it is possible to tell about someone's absurd actions while he was drunk with less risk of making him angry. Many stories about remarkably strong men are categorized by informants as tall tales, but many others, such as the present one, are offered as true stories. Steve Treat was probably the best-known strongman in north Arkansas and is said to be the prototype of one of the characters in Harold Bell Wright's highly successful novel *Shepherd of the Hills* (1907). The local character who is always looking for a handout from his friends is a familiar figure in most communities. A man addicted to tobacco but who never seems to have any of his own is primarily encountered in American folk tradition.

12. Collected by W. K. McNeil from George Vickers, Big Flat, Arkansas, 1982. Baughman's motif J1250, "Clever verbal retorts—general," is relevant.

13. Collected by George West and W. K. McNeil from Drew Bowers,

Little Rock, Arkansas, 1979, Bowers (1886–1985) was born in Randolph County, Arkansas, near Pocahontas, and spent much of his life there.

14. Collected by W. K. McNeil from Nettie Baysinger, Big Flat, Arkansas, 1982. Baughman's motif B411, "Helpful cow," is applicable. The most famous appearance of this motif is, of course, in the Cinderella story, but that cow is a supernatural animal. There is, however, a supernatural quality about this story, for the animal appeared only when the family needed her.

15. Collected by W. K. McNeil from Julie Kelley, Big Flat, Arkansas, 1982.

16. Collected by W. K. McNeil from Commodore Rose, Big Flat, Arkansas, 1982.

17. Collected by W. K. McNeil from Nola Treat, Big Flat, Arkansas, 1982. In several respects Treat's tale is an example of the typical jayhawker story, the two notable exceptions being that no one is killed and the boy in fact, escapes. Baughman's motif R200, "Escapes and pursuits," is relevant.

18. Collected by W. K. McNeil from Nettie Baysinger, Big Flat, Arkansas, 1982. Baughman's motifs R10, "Abductions," and S260, "Sacrifices," apply.

19. Collected by W. K. McNeil from Randolph Boyd, Big Flat, Arkansas, 1982. Baughman's motifs L102, "Unpromising heroine," and L160, "Success of the unpromising hero (heroine)," apply.

20. Collected by W. K. McNeil from Commodore Rose, Big Flat, Arkansas, 1982. Baughman's motifs K500, "Escape from death or danger by deception," K520, "Death escaped through disguise, shamming, or substitution," and K1810, "Deception by disguise" apply.

21. Collected by W. K. McNeil and George West from Coy Logan, Berryville, Arkansas, 1979. Metalton is a community twelve miles south of Berryville. Logan (1906–1981) spent over forty years as a teacher and school administrator in Carroll County, Arkansas. He developed a keen interest in local history when he was a student at Arkansas Tech in Russellville in 1930 and did a paper for a history seminar that included his own retellings of narratives he had learned from his grandmother and her older contemporaries. Logan can be heard telling this jayhawker story on the LP *Not Far From Here*.

22. Collected by W. K. McNeil from Matilda Morrow, Big Flat, Arkansas, 1982. Baughman's motifs R200, "Escapes and pursuits," and R300, "Refuges and recaptures," are relevant.

23. Collected by W. K. McNeil and George West from Carroll Hancock, Hasty, Arkansas, 1979. The legend of the Indian's hidden treasure has been in Hancock's family for four generations. Baughman's motifs N500, "Treasure trove," and N512, "Treasure in underground chamber

(cavern)," are relevant. Hancock can be heard telling his legend on *Not Far From Here*.

24. Collected by W. K. McNeil from George Vickers, Big Flat, Arkansas, 1982. Baughman's general motif A1617, "Origin of place name," applies here and to the next text.

25. Collected by W. K. McNeil from Julie Kelley, Big Flat, Arkansas, 1982.

26. Collected by James Johnson from a thirty-two-year-old woman in Clarksville, Arkansas, identified only as M. Dickerson, 1988.

27. Collected by James Johnson from a woman identified only as D. Plugge, Clarksville, Arkansas, 1988.

28. Collected by James Johnson from C. Rice, Clarksville, Arkansas, who was thirty-nine years old at the time of collection, 1988. In *The Choking Doberman and Other "New" Urban Legends* (New York and London: W. W. Norton & Company, 1984), p. 78, Jan Brunvand says that the legend presented in texts 26–28 is one of the pervasive modern horror legends with the best documented early history.

29. Collected by W. K. McNeil from Hubert Wilkes, Cave City, Arkansas, 1979. Wilkes (1905–1984) was one of my best informants. Fortunately, his son, Barry, is keeping the folktale tradition alive in the Wilkes family.

30. Collected by W. K. McNeil from George Vickers, Big Flat, Arkansas, 1982. Baughman's motif X1286.2.1.1, "Mosquitoes eat cow, ring bell to call calf," applies to this and the preceding two texts.

31. Collected by W. K. McNeil and George West from Toby Treat, Big Flat, Arkansas, 1982. Baughman's motif X1205.1 (g), "Small wooden object struck by snake swells so that man cuts great quantity of lumber from it," applies.

32. Collected by W. K. McNeil and George West from Toby Treat, Big Flat, Arkansas, 1982. The motifs J1700, "Absurd ignorance," and J1732, "Ignorance of certain foods," apply.

33. Collected by W. K. McNeil from Hubert Wilkes, Cave City, Arkansas, 1979. Wilkes can be heard telling this tale on *Not Far From Here*. Baughman assigns this Type 1951, "Is wood split?" and also cites it as motif W111.5.10.1.

34. Collected by George West from Dr. William Hudson, Jasper, Arkansas, 1979. Dr. Hudson (1891–1990) was a noted research doctor and medical scientist who returned to his native Jasper after retiring in 1961. Many of his stories, such as this one, concerned his Uncle Will, a familiar figure in the community in earlier generations. This is Baughman's Type 1920, "Contest in lying."

35. Collected by W. K. McNeil and George West from Elisha Honey-

cutt, Big Flat, Arkansas, 1982. Baughman's motif J1761, "Animal thought to be object," applies.

36. Collected by W. K. McNeil and George West from Trisha Haffner, Big Flat, Arkansas, 1982. This tale is not included as either a type or motif by Baughman, but a version does appear in *Tomatoes in the Tree Top*, a collection of tall tales associated with Harry Rhine (1883–1962), a man known as the "biggest liar in Tishomingo County, Mississippi."

37. Collected by W. K. McNeil from Hubert Wilkes, Cave City, Arkansas, 1979. Baughman lists this as Type 1889Lm, "Lie: the split dog."

Anyone interested in learning more about Ozark folklore should begin a search for titles with the excellent two-volume *Ozark Folklore: An Annotated Bibliography*. Both volumes were compiled and edited by Vance Randolph; the first was originally published in 1972, done by Randolph alone. In the preparation of the second volume, published in 1987 by the University of Missouri press in a set with the republished first volume, Randolph was greatly assisted by Gordon McCann, who did a majority of the entries and got the manuscript ready for publication after Randolph's death in 1980. These two books, which constitute the best published folklore bibliography from any American region, discuss a majority of the publications on Ozark folklore that appeared in print through 1982. Because *Ozark Folklore: An Annotated Bibliography* is so thorough and has such extensive commentary for entries, my remarks here will be confined mainly to works that have been published since 1982.

Two magazines that are a valuable resource for anyone interested in Ozark culture are *The Ozarks Mountaineer* and *Bittersweet*. The *Mountaineer* founded in 1952 by Roscoe Stewart, was edited for over twenty-five years by Clay Anderson; since his death in 1993 Gerald Dupy has been the editor. A popular magazine written in a nonacademic style, the *Mountaineer* has numerous articles on topics that are otherwise little discussed in print. The magazine's value for folklorists is that most of the articles are based on detailed interviews with traditional craftsmen and musicians. *Bittersweet*, which was produced by students at the Lebanon, Missouri, high school from 1973 to 1983, is now defunct. Like *Foxfire*, the magazine that influenced it, *Bittersweet* was very nostalgic and presented materials that are widespread as though they were unique to the Ozarks. Nevertheless, the magazine did contain much valuable firsthand material on Ozark folklore and popular culture, and it was generally better written than *Foxfire*. A similar publication is now being produced at the high school in West Plains, Missouri.

Probably the first serious collector of Ozark folk traditions was the indefatigable Silas C. Turnbo (1844–1925), who spent over forty years amassing interviews dealing with Ozark folklife. During his lifetime he received little acclaim for his efforts, but his important work is gaining official notice now, seventy years after his death. In 1987 genealogist Desmond Walls Allen published five volumes under the title *Turnbo's Tales of the Ozarks* through her Arkansas Research imprint. Allen provided little in the way of annotations or editorial comment but did include a detailed index with each volume. More recently, Lynn Morrow and James Keefe published a heavily annotated selection from the Turnbo Papers under the title *White River Chronicles* (Fayetteville: University of Arkansas Press, 1994). Earlier, the same editors performed a similar service with their *A Connecticut Yankee in the Frontier Ozarks* (Columbia: University of Missouri Press, 1988), a selection from the writings of Theodore Pease Russell (1820–1899) who, for many years, wrote a newspaper column titled "Old Times."

Among the numerous Ozark guidebooks, most are of a superficial nature, with texts that sound as if they were written by chamber of commerce members. An exception is Phyllis Rossiter's *A Living History of the Ozarks* (Gretna, La.: Pelican, 1992), a mammoth and worthwhile guidebook that contains fair assessments of sites throughout the Ozarks and includes a great deal of information about local history. Although like most guidebooks it is liberally illustrated with photos, it is unusual in that many of the pictures are not standard publicity shots. The book is not flawless but will most likely stand up to the test of time.

While there is no comprehensive work on Ozark folk architecture, Jean Sizemore's *Ozark Vernacular Houses: A Study of Rural Homeplaces in the Arkansas Ozarks 1830–1930* (Fayetteville: University of Arkansas Press, 1994) is an admirable discussion of the folk architecture of one part of the Ozarks. Sarah Brown's article, "Folk Architecture in Arkansas," in W. K. McNeil and William M. Clements, *An Arkansas Folklore Sourcebook* (Fayetteville: University of Arkansas Press, 1992) is also useful, and, because it is written for a popular, rather than an academic audience, is probably the best place for a novice in folk architecture to begin searching for information. Paul Faris's *Ozark Log Cabin Folks: The Way They Were* (Little Rock: Rose Publishing Co., 1983) is a nostalgic but useful examination of one aspect of Arkansas Ozark folk architecture. The book is valuable because Faris wisely not only made a photographic record of the cabins but gathered much information about the people who built them and lived in them.

Neither is there a comprehensive work on Ozark crafts, but a helpful source of information on early crafts activity is Swannee Bennett's and William B. Worthen's first volume of *Arkansas Made* (Fayetteville: University of Arkansas Press, 1990), a survey of furniture making, quilting, silversmithing, pottery, and gun making in the state before 1870. While the book deals mainly with non-Ozark materials, it does provide considerable information on Ozark craftsmen active in those five types of work.

It is particularly noteworthy for excellent photos of many of the items discussed in the text.

Earl Schrock's "Traditional Arkansas Foodways" in McNeil and Clements, *An Arkansas Folklore Sourcebook*, concentrates on the Arkansas Ozarks and is both the most recent and the best published work on the topic. There is other information in this volume as well that will be useful to anyone interested in Ozark folklore. While the editors made an effort to cover a broader area than just the Arkansas Ozarks, the history of past folklore work in Arkansas, most of which has been done in the Ozarks, and the fact that most professional folklorists currently active in Arkansas are in that portion of the state meant that much of the text focuses on the Ozarks.

Nothing has supplanted Vance Randolph's four-volume *Ozark Folksongs* (originally Columbia; State Historical Society of Missouri, 1946–1950; reissued by Columbia: University of Missouri Press, 1980), and it is doubtful that anything will in the near future. That feat will be achieved only when the massive collection of folksongs accumulated by Max Hunter, which now exists only in archive form in the Springfield, Missouri, public library and in other depositories around the United States, is published. At present no one is working to make that project a reality. My own *Southern Folk Ballads* (Little Rock: August House, 1987-1988) and *Southern Mountain Folksongs* (Little Rock: August House, 1993) contain much Ozark material. My *Ozark Mountain Humor* (Little Rock: August House, 1989) is a survey of a topic not usually singled out for book-length treatment. The most important collection of Ozark humor, work done by Max Hunter, exists only in the same archives where his ballad and folksong collections are housed. My own edition of David Rattlehead, *The Life and Adventures of an Arkansaw Doctor* (Fayetteville: University of Arkansas Press, 1989), provides a glimpse at the type of humor popular in the mid-nineteenth-century Ozarks. The subject of popular entertainment in the Missouri Ozarks at the turn of the century is comprehensively treated in Robert Karl Gilmore, *Ozark Baptizings, Hangings, and Other Diversions* (Norman: University of Oklahoma Press, 1984).

James J. Johnston's *Shootin's, Obituaries, Politics; Emigratin', Socializin', Commercializin', and the Press: News Items from and About Searcy County, Arkansas 1866–1901* (Fayetteville, Arkansas: James J. Johnston, 1991) is an important but little-known book. This volume is a compilation gathered from Searcy County newspapers over a thirty-five-year period following the Civil War. Scattered throughout the book's more than four hundred pages are several references to folk customs and other aspects of folklore. Johnston added a thorough index, making the volume very usable.

Anderson, Clay. "In the Mountains." In *The Craftsman in America*. Washington, D. C.: National Geographic Society, 1975.

Arkansas Folklore. Fayetteville: The Ozark Folklore Society, 1950–1960.

Banes, Marian Tebbetts. *The Journal of Marian Tebbetts Banes*. Fayetteville, Ark.: The Washington County Historical Society, 1977.

Bauersfeld, F. S. *Tales of the Early Days*. Hollywood, Calif.: Oxford Press, 1938.

Baughman, Ernest W. *Type and Motif Index of the Folktales of England and North America*. The Hague, The Netherlands: Mouton & Co., 1966.

Bennett, Swannee, and William B. Worthen. 2 vols. *Arkansas Made: A Survey of the Decorative, Mechanical, and Fine Arts Produced in Arkansas, 1819–1870*. Fayetteville and London: The University of Arkansas Press, 1990.

Berry, Evalena. *Time and the River: A History of Cleburne County*. Little Rock: Rose Publishing Company, 1982.

Bishop, Rick. "Blacksmithing." *Bittersweet* 2, no. 3 (1975): 28–38.

Brunvand, Jan Harold. *The Choking Doberman and Other "New" Urban Legends*. New York and London: W. W. Norton & Company, Inc., 1984.

Chase, Richard. *American Folk Tales and Songs*. 1956. Reprint, New York: The New American Library of World Literature, Inc., 1962.

Child, Francis J. *The English and Scottish Popular Ballads*. 10 vols. 1882–1898. Reprint (5 vols.), New York: Dover Publications, Inc., 1965.

Deane, Ernie. *Arkansas Place Names*. Branson, Mo.: The Ozarks Mountaineer, 1986.

Dorson, Richard M. *Buying the Wind: Regional Folklore in the United States*. Chicago and London: University of Chicago Press, 1964.

Duden, Gottfried. *Report on a Journey to the Western States of North America and a Stay of Several Years Along the Missouri (During the years 1824, '25, '26, and 1827) by Gottfried Duden*. Ed. James W. Goodrich. Columbia; The State Historical Society of Missouri and the University of Missouri Press, 1980.

Garrison, Theodore. "Forty-Five Folk Songs Collected from Searcy County, Arkansas." Master's thesis, University of Arkansas, 1944.

Gerstäcker, Friedrich. *Wild Sports in the Far West*. Durham, N. C.: Duke University Press, 1968.

Gilmore, Robert Karl. *Ozark Baptizings, Hangings, and Other Diversions: Theatrical Folkways of Rural Missouri, 1885–1910*. Norman: University of Oklahoma Press, 1984.

Gunther, John. *Inside U. S. A.* New York: Harper & Brothers, 1947.

Hansen, Marcus Lee. *The Atlantic Migration 1607–1860: A History of the Continuing Settlement of the United States*. 1940. Reprint, New York: Harper & Brothers, 1961.

Harrelston, Jimmy. "I'm As Regular as a Goose A-Going Barefoot." *Bittersweet* 2, no. 3 (1975): 39–43.

Herlinger, Elizabeth. "Historical, Cultural, and Organizational Analysis of Ozarks Ethnic Identity." Ph. D. diss., University of Chicago, 1972.

Hicks, Bert, and Mildred Hicks. "Pearling on the Black River." *The Ozarks Mountaineer* 28 (1980): 52–53, 66.

Holliday, Donald R. "Autobiography of an American Family," Ph. D. diss., University of Minnesota, 1974.

Howard, Guy. *Walkin' Preacher of the Ozarks*. New York: Harper & Brothers, 1944.

Hughes, Marion. *Three Years in Arkansaw*. 1904. Reprint, Hatfield, Ark.: The Looking Glass, 1979.

Ingenthron, Elmo. *Indians of the Ozark Plateau*. Point Lookout, Mo.: School of the Ozarks Press, 1970.

Johnston, James J. *Shootin's, Obituaries, Politics; Emigratin', Socializin', Commercializin', and the Press: News Items from and About Searcy County, Arkansas 1866–1901*. Fayetteville, Ark.: James J. Johnston, 1991.

Kettelkamp, Gilbert C. "Country-School Games of the Past." *Mid-America Folklore* 8 (1980): 113–23.

Kitchens, Ben Earl. *Tomatoes in the Tree Tops: The Collected Tales of Harry Rhine*. Florence, Ala.: Thornwood Book Publishers, 1982.

Laws, G. Malcolm, Jr. *Native American Balladry: A Descriptive Study and a Bibliographical Syllabus*. Rev. ed. Philadelphia: The American Folklore Society, 1964.

McClinton, Lynn K. "The Journal of Arthur Madison Shaw." *Faulkner Facts and Fiddlings* 12 (1970).

McCord, May Kennedy. "Our Ozark Christmas Days of Long Ago." *The Ozarks Mountaineer* 2 (1953): 10.

McLeod, Walter E. *Centennial Memorial History of Lawrence County*. 1936. Reprint, Lawrence County Historical Society, 1985 (n.p.).

McNeil, W. K. *Ghost Stories from the American South*. Little Rock: August House, Inc., 1985.

———, and William M. Clements. *An Arkansas Folklore Sourcebook*. Fayetteville: University of Arkansas Press, 1992.

Mahnkey, Mary Elizabeth. "Uncle Matt, the Cooper." *Missouri Magazine* 2 (1929): 29.

Massey, Ellen Gray. *Bittersweet Country*. Garden City, N. Y.: Anchor Press/Doubleday, 1978.

Masterson, James R. *Arkansas Folklore*. 1942. Reprint, Little Rock: Rose Publishing Co., Inc., 1974.

Mills, Margie I. *Turn South for Arkansas: The Story of the Daltons of Faulkner County*. New York: Exposition Press, 1951.

Musgrave, Bonita. "A Study of the Home and Local Crafts of the Pioneers of Washington County, Arkansas." Master's thesis, University of Arkansas, 1929.

Nelson, Joseph. *Backwoods Teacher*. New York: J. B. Lippincott Co., 1949.

Not Far From Here . . . Traditional Tales and Songs Recorded in the Arkansas Ozarks, 1981. LP. Arkansas Traditions (no number).

Page, Tate C. *The Voices of Moccasin Creek*. Point Lookout, Mo.: School of the Ozarks Press, 1977.

Peel, Zillah Cross. "Old Pottery Makers of Hills Recalled." *Arkansas Gazette*, January 16, 1938.

Rafferty, Milton D. *The Ozarks: Land and Life*. Norman: University of Oklahoma Press, 1980.

Randolph, Vance. *The Ozarks: An American Survival of Primitive Society*. New York: Vanguard Press, 1931.

———. *Ozark Mountain Folks*. New York: Vanguard Press, 1932.

———. *Ozark Magic and Folklore*. 1947. Reprint, New York: Dover Publications, Inc., 1964.

———. *Sticks in the Knapsack and Other Ozark Folk Tales*. New York: Columbia University Press, 1958.

Raney, Wayne. *This Is Wayne Raney: "Life Has Not Been a Bed of Roses."* Drasco, Arkansas: L & W Publishing Company, 1990.

Rossiter, Phyllis. *A Living History of the Ozarks*. Gretna, La.: Pelican Publishing Company, 1992.

Schoolcraft, Henry Rowe. *Journal of a Tour into the Interior of Missouri and Arkansas in 1818 and 1819*. London: no publisher given, 1821.

———. *Scenes and Adventures in the Semi-Alpine Regions of the Ozark Mountains of Missouri and Arkansas*. Philadelphia: Lippincott, Grambo & Co., 1853.

Shurtleff, Harold R. *The Log Cabin Myth*. 1939, Reprint, Gloucester, Mass.: Peter Smith, 1967.

Smith, Grace Hunt. *Buttermilk and Cracklin' Bread: An Ozarks Story*. Republic, Mo.: Western Publishing Co., 1979.

Stallcup, Helene. "Candy Breaking: Country Social." *The Ozarks Mountaineer* 24 (1976): 24.

Toynbee, Arnold J. *A Study of History*. 2 vols. (abridged). New York & London: Oxford University Press, 1957.

Turnbo, Silas C. *Turnbo's Tales of the Ozarks: Biographical Sketches*. Ed. Desmond Walls Allen. Conway, Ark.: Arkansas Research, 1987.

Upton, Dell and John Michael Vlach. *Common Places: Readings in American Vernacular Architecture*. Athens, Ga.: The University of Georgia Press, 1986.

Van Horn, Donald. *Carved in Wood: Folk Sculpture in the Arkansas Ozarks*. Batesville, Ark.: Arkansas College Folklore Archive Publications, 1979.

Young, William Henry. *Buy a Broom Besom: The Story of a Broom*. Germantown, Ohio: William Henry Young, 1988.